THE LUCENT LIBRARY OF CONFLICT IN THE MIDDLE EAST

U.S. Involvement in the Middle East: Inciting Conflict

U.S. Involvement in the Middle East: Inciting Conflict

Other books in The Lucent Library of Conflict
in the Middle East series include:

The Arab-Israeli Conflict
Human Rights in the Middle East
The Middle East: An Overview
The Palestinians

THE LUCENT LIBRARY OF CONFLICT IN THE MIDDLE EAST

U.S. Involvement in the Middle East: Inciting Conflict

By Debra A. Miller

LUCENT BOOKS

An imprint of Thomson Gale, a part of The Thomson Corporation

Detroit • New York • San Francisco • San Diego • New Haven, Conn. • Waterville, Maine • London • Munich

On cover: In the spring of 2004, angry words are exchanged by U.S. soldiers and Iraqis, who are protesting the U.S. embargo of the Iraqi town of Fallujah.

Lauri Friedman, Series Editor

© 2005 Thomson Gale, a part of the Thomson Corporation.

Thomson and Star Logo are trademarks and Gale and Lucent Books are registered trademarks used herein under license.

For more information, contact
Lucent Books
27500 Drake Rd.
Farmington Hills, MI 48331-3535
Or you can visit our Internet site at http://www.gale.com

LIBRARY OF CONGRESS CATALOGING-IN-PUBLICATION DATA

Miller, Debra A.
   U.S. involvement in the Middle East: inciting conflict / by Debra A. Miller.
      p. cm. — (The Lucent library of conflict in the Middle East)
   Includes bibliographical references and index.
   ISBN 1-59018-494-7
   1. Middle East—Relations—United States—Juvenile literature. 2. United States—Relations—Middle East—Juvenile literature. I. Title. II. Title: U.S. involvement in the Middle East. III. Series: The Lucent library of conflict in the Middle East.
   DS63.2.U5M535 2004
   327.73056--dc22
                                   2004006207

Printed in the United States of America

CONTENTS

FOREWORD

On May 29, 2004, a group of Islamic terrorists attacked a housing compound in Khobar, Saudi Arabia, where hundreds of petroleum industry employees, many of them Westerners, lived. The terrorists ran through the complex, taking hostages and murdering people they considered infidels. At one point, they came across an Iraqi-American engineer who was Muslim. As the helpless stranger stood frozen before them, the terrorists debated whether or not he deserved to die. "He's an American, we should shoot him," said one of the terrorists. "We don't shoot Muslims," responded another. The militants calmly discussed the predicament for several minutes and finally came to an agreement. "We are not going to shoot you," they told the terrorized man. After preaching to him about the righteousness of Islam, they continued their bloody spree.

The engineer's life was spared because the terrorists decided that his identity as a Muslim overrode all other factors that marked him as their enemy. Among the unfortunate twenty-two others killed that day were Swedes, Americans, Indians, and Filipinos whose identity as foreigners or Westerners or, as the terrorists proclaimed, "Zionists and crusaders," determined their fate. Although the Muslim engineer whose life was spared had far more in common with his murdered coworkers than with the terrorists, in the militants' eyes he was on their side.

The terrorist attacks in Khobar typify the conflict in the Middle East today, where fighting is often done along factionalist lines. Indeed, historically the peoples of the Middle East have been unified not by national identity but by intense loyalty to a tribe, ethnic group, and above all, religious sect. For example, Iraq is home to Sunni Muslims, Shiite Muslims, Kurds, Turkomans, and Christian Assyrians who identify themselves by ethnic and religious affiliation first, and as Iraqis second. When conflict erupts, ancient, sometimes obscure alliances determine whom they fight with and whom they fight against. Navigating this complex labyrinth of loyalties is key to understanding conflict in the Middle East, because these identities generate not only passionate allegiance to one's own group but also fanatic intolerance and fierce hatred of others.

Russian author Anton Chekhov once astutely noted, "Love, friendship, respect do not unite people as much as a common hatred for something." His words serve as a slogan for conflict in the Middle East, where religious belief and tribal allegiances perpetuate strong codes of honor and revenge, and hate is used to motivate people to join in a common cause. The methods of generating hatred in the Middle East are pervasive and overt. After Friday noon prayers, for example, imams in both Sunni and Shiite mosques deliver fiery sermons that inflame tensions between the sects that run high in nearly every Muslim country where the two groups coexist. With similar intent to incite hatred, Iranian satellite television programs broadcast forceful messages to Shiite Muslims across the Middle East, condemning certain groups as threats to Shiite values.

Perhaps some of the most astounding examples of people bonding in hatred are found in the Israeli-Palestinian conflict. In the Palestinian territories, men, women, and children are consistently taught to hate Israel, and even to die in the fight for Palestine. In spring 2004, the terrorist group Hamas went so far as to launch an online children's magazine that demonizes Israel and encourages youths to become suicide bombers. On the other hand, some sectors of Israeli society work hard to stereotype and degrade Palestinians in order to harden Israelis against the Palestinian cause. Is-

raeli journalist Barry Chamish, for example, dehumanizes Palestinians when he writes, "The Palestinians know nothing of the creation of beauty, engage in no serious scholarship, pass nothing of greatness down the ages. Their legacy is purely of destruction."

This type of propaganda inflames tensions in the Middle East, leading to a cycle of violence that has thus far proven impossible to break. Terrorist organizations send suicide bombers into Israeli cities to retaliate for Israeli assassinations of Palestinian leaders. The Israeli military, in response, leads incursions into Palestinian villages to demolish blocks upon blocks of homes, shops, and schools, further impoverishing an already desperate community. To avenge the destruction and death left in the wake of the incursions, Palestinians recruit more suicide bombers to launch themselves at civilian targets in Israeli cities. Neither side is willing to let a violent attack go unreciprocated, undermining nonviolent attempts to mediate the conflict, and the vicious cycle continues.

The books in the Lucent Library of Conflict in the Middle East help readers understand this embattled region of the world. Annotated bibliographies provide readers with ideas for further research, while fully documented primary and secondary source quotations enhance the text. Each book in the series explores a different facet of conflict in the Middle East; together they provide students with a wealth of information as well as launching points for further study and discussion.

INTRODUCTION

Actions and Reactions

The eastern Mediterranean area that is generally referred to as the Middle East is roughly bordered by Turkey to the north, Egypt to the west, Afghanistan to the east, and Yemen to the south. It is usually described as including the countries or areas of Egypt, Israel, the Palestinian territories (the West Bank and the Gaza Strip), Syria, Lebanon, Jordan, Bahrain, Kuwait, Saudi Arabia, Oman, Qatar, United Arab Emirates, Iran, Iraq, Turkey, and Yemen (and is often described as including peripheral areas such as Afghanistan, Cyprus, Libya, and Pakistan).

Since the 1500s, this region has been dominated by outside powers; first, and for many centuries, by the Ottoman Empire, and after World War I by Great Britain. In recent decades America has emerged as the dominant power in the Middle East. The United States has worked to make conditions in the Middle East favorable to American interests, and this has often placed it at odds with the people of the region. This approach has led to a series of ever-more-direct American involvements in the Middle East designed to promote stability. Often, however, these policies have had unexpected consequences and contributed to conflict instead of peace.

U.S. Oil Interests

Continued access to Middle Eastern oil is one of the critical reasons for the United States to involve itself in the region. As the world's largest energy-consuming country, the United States needs a stable supply of oil to power its industry, consumer needs, and vast air- and automobile-dominated transportation system. Indeed, the discovery of oil in certain Middle Eastern areas by American companies in the 1930s was the magnet that pulled the United States into the region. Since that time, many U.S. endeavors in the region have been aimed at protecting access to this vital resource.

For example, access to oil was the main reason the United States intervened in several successive crises during the long rivalry between America and the Soviet Union that came to be known as the Cold War. The United States was determined to prevent the Soviets from gaining a foothold in the Middle East and threatening America's newly established oil concessions in Saudi Arabia as well as its interests in other oil-producing countries. This aspect of Cold War strategy was initiated by U.S. president Harry S. Truman and was continued and enhanced under the administrations of all succeeding presidents until the collapse of the Soviet Union in 1991.

Another cornerstone of U.S. foreign policy, that of supporting the nation of Israel, also became part of America's overall strategy of protecting Middle East oil. Although intended by President Truman to support Jews who had

A Middle Eastern oil well pumps thousands of gallons a day. Oil has long motivated U.S. involvement in the area.

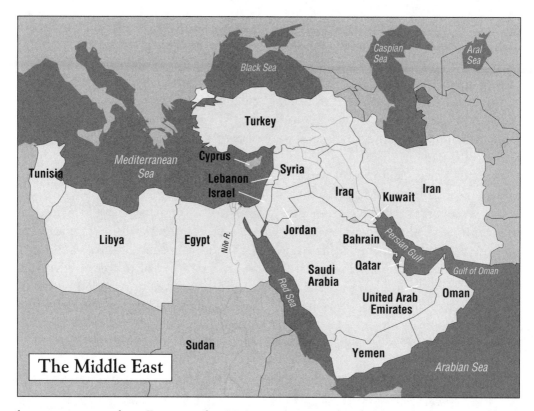

The Middle East

been persecuted in Europe, the U.S. pro-Israel policy evolved over the years into one designed to turn Israel into an arm of U.S. power in the Middle East. The United States supported Israel's political goals and strengthened its military with massive amounts of American arms and other assistance so that Israel could act as its proxy in standing off Soviet aggression in the area. A strong Israel would thus maintain regional stability and ensure U.S. access to oil.

The Price of U.S. Policies

Many of America's attempts to guide events in the Middle East have been met with suspicion and at times resistance by local inhabitants whose interests are not always served by U.S. actions. As a result, U.S. policies designed to achieve

peace and stability often have produced violence and instability instead. During the 1950s and 1960s, for example, U.S. activities in the Middle East made it an enemy of many Arab states that sought to establish indigenous Arab control over the region. In addition, America's unwavering support for Israel is believed by many to have come at the expense of neighboring Arab populations. Especially devastated by U.S. support for Israel are the Palestinians, who have been fighting for decades for the right to establish an independent Palestinian state on lands controlled by Israel. Similarly, decades of U.S. support for the shah of Iran ignored a growing fundamentalist Islamic movement in that country that finally exploded in the form of the 1979 Iranian revolution.

That same year, American hostages were taken in Iran as a symbol of that country's dissatisfaction with U.S. policies and support for an unpopular dictator there.

Today, as the world's only remaining superpower, the United States has few constraints on its activities in the Middle East. U.S. policy makers thus have undertaken military campaigns in foreign countries with and without international support. However, such actions have come with a price. Beginning with the deployment of U.S. troops to Lebanon in the early 1980s and to Saudi Arabia during the 1991 Gulf War against Iraq, for example, and more re-

cently to Afghanistan and Iraq, the United States has suffered from a rapid rise of Arab and Islamic terrorism against American targets, both abroad and at home. The attacks of September 11, 2001, are just one example of this trend, which has cost increasing numbers of American lives. Indeed, coping with the threat of terrorism has had a drastic effect on nearly all aspects of American life, and will likely continue to impact U.S. policy both at home and abroad.

So far, U.S. policies in large part have successfully met their strategic goal of keeping Middle East oil flowing for Americans. In some cases U.S. policies

Iranian revolutionaries display one of their fifty American hostages in 1979. U.S. support for the shah of Iran earned the ire of Iranians.

also have benefited its allies in the region. For example, Israel has been strengthened and protected by U.S. support, and Arab countries such as Saudi Arabia and Kuwait have acquired wealth they may never have been able to develop without U.S. investment in their oil industries. Even Iraq eventually may appreciate the U.S. overthrow of Saddam Hussein and the billions of dollars of U.S. reconstruction aid.

However, in much of the Middle East, U.S. involvement in the region is viewed negatively—as helping Israel to repress Palestinians' desires for an independent nation, often supporting corrupt Arab leaders who do not act in the best interests of their people, and generally imposing U.S. interests and desires on local populations that want to determine their own fates. It must be said, of course, that America's involvement in the Middle East is not the sole cause of turmoil in the region. With so many actors, influences, and agendas, the modern Middle East has complex problems that do not originate from any one source. However, certain U.S. policies have sowed multiple seeds of resentment, creating a chain of actions and reactions that can be very difficult to stop.

CHAPTER 1

The Roots of American Interests in the Middle East

For centuries, the Ottoman Empire ruled much of the Middle East. At its height, the Ottoman Empire stretched from the Persian Gulf to western Algeria. When the Ottomans were finally defeated in World War I, Great Britain became the dominant power in the region. It was left in charge of vast territories that had been under Ottoman control.

In the 1930s and 1940s, however, after large deposits of oil were found in various Middle East countries, America began to take an interest in the area, marking the beginning of U.S. involvement in the Middle East. These oil discoveries, together with events occurring soon after the end of World War II, led the United States to develop the three main pillars of what would become U.S. policy in the Middle East—protecting U.S. access to oil, combating Communist aggression, and supporting the nation of Israel.

British Dominance in the Middle East

Britain, a U.S. ally, preceded America as the first Western power to intrude on countries and areas in the Middle East, laying the foundation for resentments that later would be transferred to the United States. By the end of Ottoman rule, Britain had already gained influence in several areas in the region. It had created friendly relations with ruling sheikhs throughout the Persian Gulf and was well established in Egypt, where the army was led by an English general and the government was shaped by British appointees. After the defeat of the Ottomans in World War I, Great Britain also gained control over Iraq, Palestine, and Jordan (called Transjordan until 1950), while France acquired control over Lebanon and Syria. Later, Britain forced France out of Syria and

Lebanon and became the dominant power in the Middle East for several decades.

For Britain, the Middle East held great strategic importance. For one, it provided valuable oil necessary for Britain's military. It was also a base from which to defend British interests from the Soviet Union. It contained the Suez Canal, a valuable transportation route. To protect its interests, Britain forcefully suppressed Arab demands for independence. It also arbitrarily divided the region into separate states that now make up most of the Middle East—in some cases placing borders where they divided a tribal group among different states or forced enemy tribes to live in the same state.

By the end of World War II in 1945, the British were firmly entrenched in the Middle East. Britain controlled Cyprus (an island near Greece); it ruled Palestine under a mandate which gave it almost total control; and it exercised substantial influence over areas on the Oman coast and various Middle East countries, including Egypt, Syria, Lebanon, Iraq, Iran, Saudi Arabia, Kuwait, Qatar, Bahrain, and the region then known as Transjordan. Although

British troops search Arabs in 1938 Jerusalem. Britain dominated the Middle East by the end of World War II.

British Colonialism in the Middle East

The legacy of British colonialism between World War I and World War II is still felt today. The borders of many modern nations were drawn by the British during this period. The countries and governments of Egypt, Jordan, Israel, and Iraq, for example, were essentially established by Great Britain, without considering the wishes of Arab inhabitants.

In Egypt, Britain set up an independent kingdom, but one that, contrary to the desires of the population and its new king, was still largely subject to British control. Similarly, in Transjordan, British prime minister Winston Churchill appointed an Arab governor to administer the area. This system continued for many decades and later formed the borders for the modern state of Jordan.

In west Palestine, Britain resisted pleas for Arab independence, maintained control through a military occupation, and allowed European Jews to immigrate to the area—decisions that contributed to the creation of the state of Israel and to today's Israeli-Palestinian conflict. In the Persian Gulf, Britain combined incompatible Kurdish, Sunni Muslim, and Shia Muslim populations to establish the boundaries of a country that it called Iraq. Britain then imposed a colonial monarchy on the troubled area and installed a Syrian outsider, King Faisal, as head of the new nation. Iraq, and other places in the Middle East, still suffer from ethnic conflicts and political instability as a result of these historical decisions.

technically independent, these countries were ruled by leaders who were friendly with Britain and who depended on the British for economic assistance, military protection, and political support—a system that has historically been called colonialism.

By 1945 Britain had a strong military and economic presence in the region. It had over two hundred thousand troops stationed at an enormous military base along the Suez Canal in Egypt and numerous air and naval support bases spread throughout the region. Finally, the British had secured important oil reserves in Iraq, Kuwait, and Qatar, and through the Anglo-Iranian Oil Company in Iran ran the largest oil refinery in the world.

The Beginning of U.S. Oil Interests in the Middle East

British control in the Middle East was soon to be replaced by American interests. As early as the 1930s American oil companies won concessions to explore for oil in Saudi Arabia. By 1938 oil was discovered in Saudi Arabia and in Bahrain by a U.S. company called Standard Oil, and in Kuwait by another American company, Gulf Oil. As U.S. government documents at the time declared, the Middle East was "a stupendous source of strategic power, and one of the greatest material prizes in world history."[1]

U.S. policy thereafter focused on gaining and protecting American access to Middle East oil. The U.S. State

Department closely coordinated these efforts with the American oil companies and it appointed a petroleum adviser, Max Thornburg, who had ongoing ties with Standard Oil. The government also created the Petroleum Reserves Corporation, a company controlled by the State Department, to buy stock in foreign oil companies and thereby give the United States influence over the world oil market.

Saudi Arabia became the center of American oil interests. Once part of Britain's sphere of influence, the country formed close ties with America as U.S. companies invested millions to develop Saudi Arabia's oil industry. The United States controlled the production and sale of Saudi oil through a joint U.S.-Saudi company called the Arabian-American Oil Company (ARAMCO). The United States also established an important military air base at Dhahran in Saudi Arabia to protect its interests. American oil companies greatly profited from this relationship and a reliable source of oil was guaranteed for U.S. consumers.

American investments provided Saudis with enormous economic benefits as well—jobs, millions of dollars from the sale of oil, and improved health, education, transportation, and sanitation programs. As a result, Saudi king Ibn Sa'ud welcomed the relationship with America and sought U.S. protection against neighboring Arab states who envied Saudi Arabia's wealth and threatened to invade her borders. Slowly but surely, British relationships with the Saudis were being replaced by American influence.

America Intervenes in Iran

Shortly after World War II ended, another priority of U.S. Middle East policy developed: containing the Soviet Union. The Soviet Union, which during World War II was an ally of the United States, made attempts after the war to dominate surrounding countries. The United States opposed these as acts of aggression that indicated the Soviets wanted to impose their form of government—communism—onto the Middle East and other parts of the world. This struggle between the United States and the Soviets would become known as the Cold War and would last almost to the end of the twentieth century.

The first U.S. intervention in the Middle East occurred immediately after World War II when the Soviet Union tried to take control of Iran. During the war Allied troops from the United States and Britain as well as the Soviet Union were stationed in Iran with the understanding that all troops would be withdrawn at the war's end. Indeed, at a conference in 1943 all three Allied countries stated their support for Iranian independence and pledged to help rebuild Iran after the war. When the war came to a close, the American and British forces promptly left Iran.

The Soviets, however, stayed in the country. They considered control of Iran, which bordered part of the Soviet Union, to be vital to their security. The Soviet Union did not want Iran for its oil—the Soviets had their own oil reserves. Instead, the Soviets wanted to keep other countries seeking Iran's oil reserves from gaining influence so close to the Soviet border. The Soviets maintained their position in Iran by supporting various Iranian political groups, placing Communists in the Iranian government, and winning oil concessions and other rights in the country.

The United States, under the leadership of President Harry S. Truman, protested the Soviet presence in Iran. Convinced that the Soviets wanted to control the Middle East, Truman complained both directly to the Soviet Union and to the United Nations (UN) Security Council (the group of UN members who have power to determine UN actions). Truman's protests, combined with threats of U.S. military action, eventually succeeded in ousting the Soviets from Iran. Thereafter, Truman helped Iran's leader, Shah Mohammad Reza Pahlavi, to remove Communists from Iran's government and reject Soviet oil concessions.

Truman's actions laid the foundation for future American policy in Iran—a policy aimed at containing Soviet aggression, protecting a rich source of oil, and developing Iran as a U.S. ally and a vital part of America's northern Middle East security. Indeed, the Iran policy set the pattern for U.S. Mideast policy throughout the twentieth century, in which the United States supported foreign leaders simply because they opposed communism and regardless of whether or not they were corrupt and brutal. This caused widespread resentment against the United States among the Arab people.

The Truman Doctrine

Following the Soviet attempt to expand into Iran, the United States continued to oppose Communist aggression in the region. The next test of this policy came in 1947 in Turkey and Greece. Soviet leader Joseph Stalin sought control over the Dardanelles, an important waterway under Turkish control, and claimed parts of Turkey which he said historically belonged to the Soviet Union. To secure these interests, the Soviets in the spring of 1947 built up their troops along the Turkish-Soviet border. At the same time as the Soviets were pushing to gain control of Turkish areas, they also tried to take over the government in Greece.

President Truman saw the matter as a crisis that threatened to give the Soviets an inroad to the Middle East. He thus developed a policy that became known as the Truman Doctrine. Announced in a 1947 message to the U.S. Congress, the doctrine described the situation in Greece and Turkey as a struggle between the U.S. ideals of freedom and democracy and the repressive government rule favored by communism. Truman pledged to "assist free people to work out their own destinies in their own way."[2] As part of the doctrine, Truman requested and received congressional authorization to send $400 million in U.S. economic and military aid to Greece and Turkey to help them resist Soviet pressure. With this support, order was restored in both countries and the Communist influence was blocked.

The Truman Doctrine became a turning point in U.S. foreign and Middle

The shah of Iran parades in Tehran after his coronation. The United States supported the shah; the shah in turn protected U.S. oil and political interests.

The Truman Doctrine

On March 12, 1947, President Harry S. Truman outlined what would become known as the "Truman Doctrine" in an address before a joint session of Congress. In the speech, after explaining the crises developing in Greece and Turkey, Truman said:

At the present moment in world history nearly every nation must choose between alternative ways of life. The choice is too often not a free one.

One way of life is based upon the will of the majority, and is distinguished by free institutions, representative government, free elections, guarantees of individual liberty, freedom of speech and religion, and freedom from political oppression.

The second way of life is based upon the will of a minority forcibly imposed upon the majority. It relies upon terror and oppression, a controlled press and radio; fixed elections, and the suppression of personal freedoms.

I believe that it must be the policy of the United States to support free peoples who are resisting attempted subjugation by armed minorities or by outside pressures.

I believe that we must assist free peoples to work out their own destinies in their own way.

I believe that our help should be primarily through economic and financial aid which is essential to economic stability and orderly political processes. . . .

I therefore ask the Congress to provide authority for assistance to Greece and Turkey in the amount of $400,000,000 for the period ending June 30, 1948. . . .

The seeds of totalitarian regimes are nurtured by misery and want. They spread and grow in the evil soil of poverty and strife. They reach their full growth when the hope of a people for a better life has died. We must keep that hope alive.

The free peoples of the world look to us for support in maintaining their freedoms.

If we falter in our leadership, we may endanger the peace of the world—and we shall surely endanger the welfare of our own nation.

President Harry Truman's foreign policy set the tone for U.S. involvement in the Middle East.

East policy. During World War II the United States had largely accommodated the Soviets as an American ally. After the war, however, Truman's policy was to make the United States the leader of the free world and an enemy of the Soviets wherever they tried to expand their influence. As Truman said in his memoirs, "Wherever [Communist] aggression, direct or indirect, threatened the peace, the security of the United States was involved."[3] The doctrine set the stage for America's decades-long anti-Communist policy in the Middle East, and it would be used, again and again, as a justification for U.S. involvement in the region.

The Question of Palestine

Another aspect of early U.S. policies in the Middle East, both during and after World War II, involved support for the immigration of European Jews to an Arab-populated area near the Mediterranean Sea called Palestine. Jews from Europe began settling in Palestine to escape anti-Jewish persecution (called anti-Semitism) in the late 1800s, when the region was still part of the Ottoman Empire. Eventually, Jews from around the world created a movement (called Zionism) to establish Israel, the biblical home of the Jews, as a permanent homeland for the Jewish people. Britain, which controlled Palestine after World War I, encouraged Jews to immigrate, believing their presence would improve the area economically for both Jews and Palestinian Arabs. Arabs, however, resented the influx of non-Arabs, leading to fighting between the two groups.

After the war the United States became involved in the issue. President Woodrow Wilson was then promoting national self-determination—the right of people to govern themselves. At President Wilson's suggestion, the allied nations of France, Great Britain, Russia, and the United States in 1919 set up a commission, called the King-Crane Commission, to investigate the situation in Palestine. The commission concluded that Arabs wanted their own country and recommended independence for Palestine. If independence could not be accomplished, the commission recommended that the United States supervise Palestine and that Jewish immigration be slowed.

The allied powers met again in 1920 at a conference in San Remo, Italy. Instead of following the recommendations of the commission, however, they rejected Palestinian independence and gave Britain control over Palestine. British rule was made official in 1922 when it was granted a mandate (official authority to administer the territory) by the League of Nations, an international body created after World War I to promote peace and security. As Middle East analyst B.J. Smith explains, "The assignment of territory under the mandate system was little more than a thinly disguised title deed"[4] that gave Britain virtually complete control over the future of Palestine. The interests of Arabs, who at that time constituted approximately 90 percent of the population, were largely ignored. As a result, under British rule Jewish immigration to Palestine increased dramatically. By 1936 almost

European Jewish immigrants arrive in Palestine in 1929. U.S. support of Jewish immigration to Palestine angered Arab residents.

four hundred thousand Jews resided in Palestine, making up about 30 percent of the area's population.

U.S. Support for Jewish Immigration to Palestine

These changes in Palestine were resisted bitterly by Arabs living in and near the area. Indeed, tensions between local Arabs and Jewish immigrants arose in the 1880s when the first Jewish settlements were established. Tensions increased through the years; by the early twentieth century, Arab demonstrations had erupted in various Arab cities throughout the Middle East and riots

and violence broke out in Palestine. In the 1930s the Arabs became more organized and began an armed struggle against both the Jewish settlers and the British. The rebellion was so effective and widespread that the British in 1938 were forced to send many thousands of additional British troops to the region to contain the violence.

In response to the escalating tensions, the British in 1939 issued a policy statement called the White Paper, which reversed their pro-Zionist policy and restricted Jewish immigration. However, this restriction came at one of the most critical times for Jews: the beginning of World War II and the Holocaust (Nazi Germany's program of persecution and extermination which killed approximately 6 million Jews throughout Europe). The horror of the Holocaust made the Zionist movement even more committed to building a Jewish homeland in Palestine. To this end, Jews began to resist British control of Palestine. Jewish terrorist groups such as the Irgun Zva'i Le'umi and the Stern Gang attacked British troops and offices, trying to force Britain out of Palestine. As the violence and terrorism mounted, Britain began to search for a solution.

In the United States President Harry Truman felt great sympathy for the plight of Jewish survivors of the Holocaust. He also was lobbied by Jewish leaders in the United States for help with the Zionist cause. The president thus became closely involved with the issue of Palestine; he urged Britain to lift restrictions on Jewish immigration to Palestine. Truman's actions reversed President Wilson's previous support for Arab independence. Now, U.S. policy was to support the Jewish Zionists who wanted a homeland in Palestine; this idea would become a central part of U.S. Middle East policy from this point onward.

Jewish corpses lie stacked on a wagon in a Nazi death camp. The Holocaust garnered worldwide sympathy for the plight of the Jews.

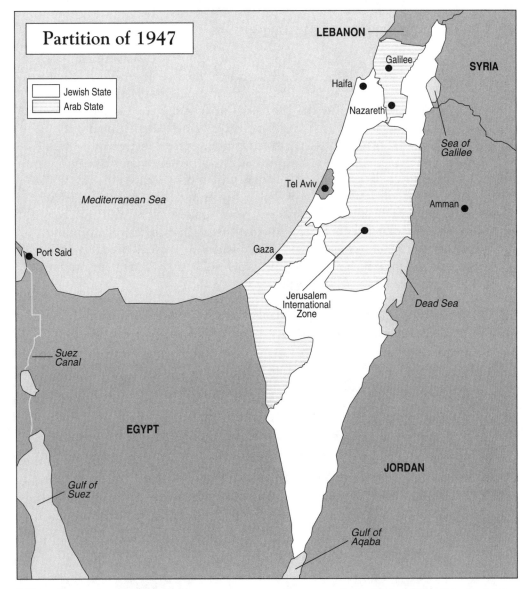

Partition of 1947

Jewish State
Arab State

LEBANON

Galilee

SYRIA

Haifa

Nazareth

Sea of Galilee

Mediterranean Sea

Tel Aviv

Amman

Gaza

Port Said

Jerusalem International Zone

Dead Sea

Suez Canal

EGYPT

JORDAN

Gulf of Suez

Gulf of Aqaba

The Creation of Israel

The growing violence in Palestine and the increasing cost of maintaining troops in the area at a time when the British economy was already weak from war finally led Britain to get out of Palestine. In January 1947 Britain turned the matter over to the United Nations, a new international organization created after World War II to replace the League of Nations. The United Nations set up a Special Committee on Palestine (UNSCOP), which recommended that Palestine be granted independence. The majority of UNSCOP members recommended that the region be split into separate Jewish and Arab nations, with Jerusalem as an international city. A minority, however, thought this partition plan was unworkable and

The Palestinian Refugees

During the creation of Israel in 1948 approximately 750,000 Palestinian Arabs, or about 75 percent of the native Arab population in Palestine, fled from the Arab areas occupied by Israel to refugee camps in neighboring Arab states. The refugee exodus continued after the 1967 Six-Day War, in which Israel seized additional Arab lands, and resulted in about 300,000 more Palestinian refugees.

Since then, the population of Palestinian refugees in the Middle East has grown to about 5 million. About half of them live in thirty-two poverty-stricken refugee camps located in Jordan, Syria, and Lebanon. Others have escaped the camps and resettled in other areas. The right of these refugees to return to their homelands has become one of the most difficult issues in the Arab-Israeli conflict. The Palestinians insist that refugees must be allowed to return and be paid compensation, while Israel says it has no room for 5 million additional people. Indeed, large numbers of Palestinians returning to lands in Israel would give Arabs a majority and change Israel from a Jewish to an Arab state.

A Palestinian woman grieves over her lost home which was destroyed by Israeli soldiers. Palestinian refugees now number about 5 million.

proposed that Palestine be kept united as a collection of self-governing Arab and Jewish states.

Jewish leaders accepted UNSCOP's majority recommendation for partition; but Arabs rejected both the majority and minority reports. The Arab League, in fact, threatened war if the United Nations accepted either report. The Arabs wanted all of Palestine to be declared an independent Arab nation.

On November 29, 1947, the UN General Assembly passed Resolution 181, voting overwhelmingly in favor of partitioning Palestine. As a result of widespread sympathy for the post-Holocaust plight of the Jews, Resolution 181 was drafted in their favor. Jews, who made up 31 percent of the Palestinian population, were awarded 55 percent of the land; Arab Palestinians were awarded about 45 percent. Not surprisingly, the resolution was vehemently opposed by all Arab and Islamic countries. President Truman supported and actively promoted the partition resolution.

Arab groups angered by the outcome of the vote refused to accept partition, and a civil war broke out in Palestine. The fighting continued until May 14, 1948, when Britain officially terminated the mandate and abruptly pulled its forces out of Palestine. At 4:00 P.M. that same day, Israel declared its independence. The following day, the new nation of Israel was attacked by five Arab states—Egypt, Jordan, Syria, Lebanon, and Iraq.

The ensuing war, known in Israel as the War of Independence, was decisively won by Israel. For Palestinians, however, the war was a disaster. Israel not only successfully defended all of the territory awarded to it by the United Nations but also seized part of the territory that had been awarded to the Palestinians. Jordan and Egypt seized the remaining Palestinian areas of East Palestine and Gaza. The Palestinians were left with virtually no land they could call their own. Even worse, the war created about 750,000 Palestinian refugees, who fled from their homes in the territories conquered by Israel to other Arab countries and parts of Palestine that came under Arab control.

The United States Supports the New State of Israel

The United States recognized the state of Israel eleven minutes after it proclaimed its independence. America also immediately began providing financial support for Israel, granting the new country a $100 million loan. Truman's decision to support a Jewish state in Palestine was made against the advice of the U.S. State Department and many U.S. foreign policy experts, who were concerned about the impact on U.S.-Arab relations. As Truman himself stated in his memoirs, "The Department of State's specialists on the Near East were, almost without exception, unfriendly to the idea of a Jewish State."[5] These experts warned the president that supporting the partition would create anti-American sentiment in the Arab world.

However, as would often be the case in future Middle East policy, the president was primarily concerned about the votes he might lose if he did not support Zionism. As Truman explained at the time during a meeting with U.S. ambassadors to the Middle East, "I'm sorry gentlemen, but I have to answer to hundreds of thousands [of Jews] who are anxious for the success of Zionism: I do not have hundreds of thousands of Arabs among my constituents [that is, voting Americans]."[6] Also, as Mideast policy expert Sheldon L. Richman points out, "support for Jewish . . . statehood in

Palestine . . . sidestepped the sensitive issue of U.S. immigration quotas, which had kept European Jews out of the United States since the 1920s and had left many of them at the mercy of the Nazis [the German political party that perpetrated the Holocaust]."[7] In other words, the U.S. support for a Jewish state may have been a convenient way to support Zionism without allowing Jews to immigrate to the United States.

As many predicted, U.S. support for the creation of Israel alienated Arabs and set the tone for U.S.-Arab relations for decades to come. Arabs saw the UN vote as a wholly unfair allocation of Arab lands and a manipulation of Arab inter-ests by larger and more powerful countries. As Evan M. Wilson, assistant chief of the State Department's Division of Near Eastern Affairs during the Truman years, later wrote, "It is no exaggeration to say that our relations with the entire Arab world have never recovered from the events of 1947–48 when we sided with the Jews against the Arabs."[8]

In any case, supporting Israel became an important part of U.S. Middle East policy. Later, the U.S. relationship with Israel would deepen. Israel would become a strategic ally and guard against Soviet influence in the Middle East, which would help protect U.S. oil interests in the region.

CHAPTER 2

America as the Dominant Middle East Power

In the 1950s, under the leadership of President Dwight D. Eisenhower, the United States completely replaced Britain as the dominant power in the Middle East. This process began when British control over various parts of the region began to decline, leaving the United States and the Soviet Union in a struggle for dominance in the region. Revolts against British influence in Iran and Egypt and a civil war in Lebanon had left these areas unstable and vulnerable to outside influences. The United States, to block Soviet expansionism, intervened to maintain U.S. influence. These interventions formed the foundation for future American alliances and policies in the region.

The Mosaddeq Oil Crisis in Iran

One of the first crises to arise in the Middle East during this period began in 1951 in Iran. A group within the Iranian government led by Mohammad Mosaddeq complained that Iran was not receiving a large enough share of the profits from the British-controlled Anglo-Iranian Oil Company (AIOC). Mosaddeq also wanted to oust the British from Iran altogether. To this end, he began pressuring the pro-Western Iranian king, Shah Mohammad Reza Pahlavi (whom the United States had helped elevate to power in the 1940s), to nationalize Iran's oil industry. Mosaddeq succeeded and Iran took over the oil company's operations on May 2, 1951. This gave Iran full control over its oil production and sales. Thereafter, Mosaddeq, who became Iran's prime minister, used the Iranian army to take over a major oil refinery previously controlled by Britain, expelled British personnel from the country, and ended

Mohammad Mosaddeq ousted the British from Iran and took over its oil production in 1951.

Although the nationalization of its oil industry had been a victory for Iran, it also had great consequences. Soon all the major oil companies, in solidarity with AIOC, refused to buy Iranian oil. As a result, Iran's oil production came to an almost complete halt as companies purchased oil from Saudi Arabia, Iraq, and Kuwait. The lack of oil revenues soon led to an economic crisis in Iran.

At first the United States sought to remain neutral in the crisis. Soon, however, American policy makers became very concerned about the disruption of world oil supplies. They were also worried that the Soviets would try to gain control of Iran, as they had tried to do once before following World War II. Indeed, the world had just witnessed in 1950 a clear example of Soviet aggression in Korea that led to the Korean War, and the United States was on guard against the Soviets next trying to move into the Middle East. Iran's government, in fact, already included a group of Communists who were sponsored by the Soviets and who were poised to take advantage of Iran's instability to try to gain control of the country. For these reasons, the United States intervened to try to resolve the conflict, sending an envoy to Iran to search for political solutions. Meanwhile, the political climate in Iran became highly charged, as mobs protested against the British and Prime Minister Mosaddeq rejected numerous American mediation proposals and sought to wrest power from the shah.

diplomatic relations between Iran and Britain. Mosaddeq had challenged Britain and won.

Mosaddeq's actions created a crisis for Britain because Iran had been its primary source of oil. Although Britain tried to fight Iran's action and complained to the UN Security Council and the World Court, none of these efforts produced a solution satisfactory to the British. Indeed, the World Court in 1952 refused to consider Britain's claim.

By the time Dwight Eisenhower became president in 1953, Mosaddeq had gained substantial control over the Iranian military and the government, reducing the shah's power significantly. Ultimately, when Mosaddeq refused to negotiate his oil policy, the United States and Britain planned a covert U.S. operation to remove him from power. The overthrow plan, prepared by the Central Intelligence Agency (CIA), was justified as necessary to contain the Soviet threat to the Middle East; the United States was convinced

The Cold War

The end of World War II resulted in a rivalry between the United States and the Soviet Union which came to be known as the Cold War. The United States and the Soviet Union each promoted a different political system. The United States promoted the idea of democracy, in which people choose leaders through free elections and property is held by private individuals and companies. The Soviets employed the system of communism, in which an authoritarian government completely controls goods and property and distributes them, equitably (in an ideal world), to the people. During the Cold War, the superpowers competed for influence around the world, trying to spread their beliefs to other countries.

This period also witnessed the development of sophisticated nuclear weapons that made the competition between the United States and the Soviets very dangerous. Both countries knew that if they ever engaged in a general war with each other, it could lead to the use of nuclear weapons capable of destroying much of the planet. Both sides, therefore, avoided direct confrontations with the other, but tried to exert influence in various areas of the world by sending military and economic aid to other countries. With the two superpowers competing in this manner, smaller countries and emerging nations felt compelled to align themselves with either the Americans or the Soviets as a means of acquiring aid and promoting their own futures. They usually, however, became pawns in the games of greater powers.

The Soviets display their military strength in a parade during the Cold War era.

that Mosaddeq was sliding Iran toward Soviet control. As the U.S. secretary of state John Foster Dulles explained at the time, "If [the Soviets] could control Iran, they would control the Persian Gulf. This has been their dream, their chief ambition, ever since the days of Peter the Great [emperor of Russia in the late 1600s and early 1700s]."[9]

After consultations with the shah, American agents were sent into Iran to help topple Mosaddeq and replace him with someone loyal to the shah, a general named Fazlollah Zahedi. On August 10, 1953, the shah signed papers dismissing Mosaddeq and installing Zahedi. Mosaddeq, however, defied the shah's orders to step down and encouraged pro-Communist rioting among the Iranian people. Ultimately, the shah won after a group of anti-Mosaddeq Iranians also took to the streets along with army units loyal to the shah. In the end, Mosaddeq was captured, his forces were dispersed, and the shah resumed full power in Iran.

The crisis in Iran and the U.S. plot to return the shah to power was a triumph for the United States, but it effectively ended British dominance there. Indeed, although Britain insisted that the AIOC return as sole operator of the Iran oil fields, U.S. negotiators managed to get the British to reduce their share of Iranian oil and give U.S. oil companies access to Iranian oil reserves previously controlled by Britain. Accordingly, in 1954 a new oil agreement was negotiated that gave five American oil companies—Standard Oil of New Jersey (now Exxon), Socony

Vacuum (now Mobil), Standard Oil of California (now Chevron), Texaco, and Gulf—a 40 percent share of Iranian oil profits.

The United States thus vigorously asserted its influence in Iran to make certain that the flow of oil from the country would benefit the United States. It also demonstrated its dedication to preventing the Soviets from getting a foothold in the country. Thereafter, the United States became the primary source of millions of dollars of economic and other aid to the shah, beginning a long period of close Iranian-American relations that would last until the Iranian Islamic revolution in 1979.

The United States Courts Egypt

A second anti-British crisis emerged in the Middle East in Egypt. Like the Iranians who supported Mosaddeq's rebellion against the British, many Egyptians were tiring of the British exercising so much control over their country. Indeed, all over the world, British colonialism was on the decline, as people in various British colonies and protectorates around the world rose up against British rule.

Following this pattern, in July 1952 revolutionaries overthrew Egypt's government, ousting the country's pro-British leader, King Farouk. They were led by army general Gamal Abdel Nasser, who became Egypt's new president. Nasser's goal was to rid Egypt of all British influence and unify Arab nations in the Middle East. This movement, known as Pan-Arabism, sought

During the Cold War, the Soviet Union and the United States competed for control of Iranian oil wells like this one.

to increase Arab political power and so decrease British and American influence throughout the region.

The main focus of Nasser's anti-British campaign in Egypt was Britain's huge military base along the Suez Canal—an area sixty-five miles long and three miles wide that housed approximately eighty thousand British soldiers. Nasser demanded that Britain withdraw all its troops from this Egyptian base. Britain, however, was reluctant to do this. The Suez Canal was important to Britain and many other countries as an international shipping route and the base protected the canal and other British interests in the region. In addition, Britain had just withdrawn from Palestine, its only other suitable military base in the Middle East, making the Suez base even more important to the British. Britain thus sought the help of the United States to negotiate an arrangement with Egypt that would allow it to maintain its base there.

Initially, Truman was still president of the United States and supported a British proposal for solving the Suez crisis. When Dwight D. Eisenhower became president in 1953, however, he saw things differently. Eisenhower disagreed with Britain's policy of treating Middle Eastern countries as colonies. Instead, he believed it was necessary to support rising Arab nationalism, that is, Arab demands for independence, because strong and independent Arab nations were the best defense against Soviet expansionism. He thought that weak nations, on the other hand, would be prey to Communist takeover. In addition, many at the U.S. State Department considered Egypt, one of the largest Middle East countries, as key to

Egyptian president Gamal Abdel Nasser delivers a speech in 1960. Egypt's Middle East leadership role made it an important U.S. ally.

blocking Soviet influence and protecting U.S. interests in the region.

The United States, therefore, adopted a pro-Egypt policy. Ultimately, by pressuring Britain, the United States was able to mediate the dispute and negotiate a final agreement in October 1954 that provided for withdrawal of British troops from the Suez base. The agreement also provided for freedom of navigation to all countries on the Suez Canal, maintenance of the Suez base by Egyptian and British technicians, and overflight and landing rights for Britain. Finally, the deal allowed Britain to reactivate its base in the event of an attack on any Arab state (and/or Turkey) by any non-Arab state (such as the Soviet Union). As a result of losing Egypt, the British moved their main military Middle East headquarters to Cyprus.

The Suez incident marked a major shift in U.S. Middle East policy. In the past, the United States had often relied on and supported British influence in the Mideast. The rebellion in Egypt, however, had placed the United States squarely at odds with Britain's policies and moved America into a more direct role in the area. For example, the United States quickly became the major arms supplier to Egypt, a role previously held by Britain. Like the Iranian oil crisis, therefore, the event demonstrated Britain's decline as a Middle East power and the ascension of American influence.

The 1956 Suez Canal Crisis

The United States hoped that its efforts against Britain would encourage Egypt to become its ally. Indeed, once its independence from Britain was secured, U.S. officials hoped Egypt would assist the United States with an Arab-Israeli peace plan known as "Alpha" and join the Baghdad Pact, a U.S.-supported Middle East defense agreement.

However, U.S. attempts to befriend Egypt were ultimately unsuccessful. The United States failed to understand the depths of Arab distrust of Western powers. Because of this distrust, Egypt refused to join the Baghdad Pact and responded with little enthusiasm to the Alpha peace plan. Egypt also refused U.S. military aid because of the conditions that came with it. Suspicious of the United States, Egypt turned to the Soviet Union and in 1955 purchased a large quantity of Soviet arms. Later, Nasser took several other actions viewed in America as signs that Egypt was moving toward the Soviet Union and embracing communism. For example, he encouraged anti-British rioters in Jordan and Bahrain, spoke out against the Baghdad Pact, and bought weapons from Poland, a Communist country. Most upsetting to the United States, Nasser recognized another Communist country, the People's Republic of China.

In 1956, still hoping to win Egypt's friendship, the United States offered economic aid to finance the country's construction of the Aswan Dam. The dam project was extremely important to Nasser; it was expected to supply enough electric power to irrigate large parts of Egypt and boost the country's agricultural production. Nasser refused to accept the conditions of the American aid package, however, and tried to play the Soviets against the United States in negotiations to get a better deal. Soon, American policy makers became distrustful of Nasser's contacts with the Soviets and other Communists. Just as Egypt decided to accept the U.S. offer, U.S. secretary of state Dulles, as a result of strong congressional pressure, abruptly cancelled the deal.

The U.S. refusal to fund the dam led Nasser to nationalize, or take control of, the Suez Canal on July 26, 1956. This allowed Egypt to claim the income from operating the canal, money which Nasser claimed was needed to build the Aswan Dam. The Suez, although owned by Egypt, had been op-

The Baghdad Pact

In the early 1950s the United States began to explore the idea of developing a coalition of Middle Eastern nations to combat Soviet influence in that region. After experiencing a clear example of Soviet aggression in Korea, which led to the Korean War, the United States believed there was an increased risk that the Soviets would try to move into other areas, such as the Middle East. Initially, the United States hoped Egypt would help form a defense plan against the Soviet threat. However, Egypt's new president, Gamal Abdel Nasser, was not willing to be involved in such an undertaking.

In need of a reliable security partner for the United States, U.S. secretary of state Dulles in 1953 shifted American anti-Soviet strategic goals from Egypt to a group of northern Middle East countries. Turkey and Pakistan were approached to be the mainstays of a northern tier defense pact of states that would cooperate with the West and resist Soviet influence. The northern tier defense became a reality in February 1955 when Turkey and Iraq signed a defense agreement. In April that same year, Britain joined the pact, followed by Pakistan in September and Iran in October, making it a five-member defense pact that became known as the Baghdad Pact (because its headquarters was in Baghdad, the capital of Iraq).

After Britain joined the pact, however, the United States pulled away, declining to become part of the agreement while still encouraging Pakistan and Iran to join. The United States worried that if it joined the alliance with Britain, which then had a reputation as a colonial power in the Middle East, it would alienate other Arab states. Also, an alliance with Iraq, the main competitor with Egypt for leadership in the Arab world, would risk alienating Egypt, a country the United States was then still trying to befriend.

The Baghdad Pact was renamed the Central Treaty Organization (CENTO) in 1959, after a coup in Iraq led to Iraq's withdrawal from the pact. Treaty headquarters at that time were moved from Baghdad to Ankara, Turkey. The pact continued in force for two decades, until the 1979 revolution in Iran eventually caused its collapse.

erated by a company owned by France and Britain, which was subject to international regulations requiring the canal to be kept open to all countries in times of peace and war. Nasser's action, therefore, angered both France and Britain. Both countries wanted to use force to make Nasser return the Suez to them.

The U.S. response to Nasser's action, however, was much more muted, and the United States warned France and Britain against using force. As historian Tore T. Peterson explains, President Eisenhower felt "that as long as Nasser did not interfere with the traffic through the Canal and allowed it to operate smoothly, there was no reason to resort to force."[10]

The Suez issue soon led to open war against Egypt, not only by Britain and France, but also Israel. Israel and Egypt were already enemies that had fought an earlier war and whose relationship continued to be fractious; in addition, Nasser closed the Suez to Israeli ships. The war, which became known as the Suez-Sinai War, began on October 29, 1956, when Israel attacked Egypt and quickly seized large parts of Palestinian areas controlled by Egypt, including the Gaza Strip and the Sinai desert. France and Britain also entered the war, making air attacks on Egyptian targets.

The U.S. Response to the Suez War

The Suez-Sinai War proved to be a turning point for the United States. President Eisenhower immediately denounced the joint Israeli, British, and French action, suspended military aid to Israel, and called for a cease-fire and withdrawal of troops from Egypt. Despite the U.S. moves, however, the conflict widened when Syria entered the hostilities to help Egypt. Then, the Soviets became involved, actually threatening to send aid and forces to support Egypt in its fight against the Western powers. Finally, in November, the conflict ended when France and Britain accepted the cease-fire and withdrew, followed by Israel, which returned the territories it had captured.

The Suez crisis was significant for U.S. foreign policy because it exposed for the first time a major rift between the United States and its European allies, France and Britain. The fact that America was willing to confront its allies, France and Britain, and defend Egypt revealed how concerned the United States was about Soviet inroads in the Middle East. The Soviets by this time had already established a Communist state in North Korea and as political science professor George Lenczowski explains, "Eisenhower was determined to resist Soviet penetration into what he believed to be the most strategic area of the globe."[11]

Eisenhower took this stand because he saw the Middle East as the arena where the great confrontations of the mid–twentieth century would take place. He believed the region would be the site for the battle between communism and democracy. As such, Eisenhower was prepared to support Arab independence efforts, such as Egypt's seizure of the Suez Canal, to prevent the Soviets from gaining a foothold in the

area. As analyst Avi Shlaim notes, the Suez crisis marked the beginning of the Cold War conflict in the region: "Suez was thus an event of worldwide consequence. . . . The European phase in the history of the Middle East gave way to . . . the global rivalry and conflicting ideologies of the United States and the Soviet Union. [After the Suez Canal crisis,] the Middle East became another theater in the Cold War."[12]

Eisenhower's stance in the Suez crisis also upheld an earlier American policy of remaining impartial between Arabs and Israelis. Under the 1950 Tripartite Agreement, for example, the United States, France, and Britain agreed to limit arms supplies to Middle

Victorious Israeli troops raise their flag over the Sinai during the 1956 Suez-Sinai War. The war forced a turning point in U.S. foreign policy.

States, seeking to remain neutral and avoid an arms race, also refused a request by Israel to provide it with arms, and later, condemned its attack on Egypt. This policy of impartiality continued after the war. On the one hand, the United States condemned Israel's refusal to leave Egyptian lands in Gaza; at the same time, it reprimanded Egypt for denying Israel's right of passage in the Gulf of Aqaba and sent an American tanker to the area to defend Israeli passage.

Eastern countries to prevent any military imbalance between Israel and neighboring Arab states, and thus reduce the likelihood of open conflict in the region. The U.S. refusal to supply arms to Egypt without restrictions sought to honor this agreement, although it led Egypt to turn to the Soviet Union. Nevertheless, the United

Eisenhower's policy of neutrality did not result in closer relations with Arab nationalists, however, and this would be the last time that the United States took such a strong stance against Israel. Indeed, in spite of U.S. support for Egypt during the Suez crisis, relations between the United States and Egypt in the future would become only more strained.

The Eisenhower Doctrine

The Suez crisis had heightened U.S. concerns about Soviet expansionism in the Middle East. In 1957, in an effort to warn the Soviets against any such moves, President Eisenhower proposed and Congress authorized the use of U.S. armed forces to prevent imminent or actual aggression from Communist forces anywhere in the Middle East. This plan, which became known as the Eisenhower Doctrine, gave the United States flexibility to militarily defend all

U.S. president Dwight Eisenhower incorporated military action into U.S. Middle East policy, thereby escalating the Cold War.

nations in the region, and was one of the most significant policies of the entire Cold War.

The Eisenhower Doctrine was announced by the president in a message to Congress on January 5, 1957. Eisenhower proposed that the United States be authorized to provide assistance to Middle East nations, including "the employment of the armed forces of the United States . . . against overt armed aggression from any nation controlled by International Communism."[13] In essence, the Eisenhower Doctrine was a continuation of the Truman Doctrine, except that it authorized the use of U.S. armed forces in addition to economic and military aid. In this way, it represented a significant escalation of America's Cold War strategy.

Although many in the U.S. Congress opposed the idea as contrary to the constitutional requirement that only Congress can declare war, the doctrine was accepted in a joint congressional resolution in March. After this legislative approval, the United States also sought acceptance of the doctrine from fifteen Middle East states. Yet only Lebanon formally approved it, in return for military and economic aid. For many Arab nations, it was simply a rationale for maintaining U.S. control in the Middle East. This view was reinforced very soon, as the doctrine was employed in a number of Middle East crises.

The first test of the Eisenhower Doctrine came quickly, in April 1957, when Jordan's pro-Western government was threatened by Communist rebels. Jordan's King Hussein thwarted the at-

In the spring of 1957 angry pro-communist demonstrators in Amman, Jordan, protest the Eisenhower Doctrine and Jordan's pro-Western government.

tempted coup, however, by dismissing two army chiefs of staff who betrayed him, and reestablishing control of the country. The United States, in accordance with the Eisenhower Doctrine, sent the U.S. Navy's Sixth Fleet to the area to support Hussein and granted Jordan $10 million in economic aid. This grant later evolved into an annual payment, eventually replacing British aid and influence in yet another Arab country. In Jordan, communism was defeated and America expanded its influence.

The Eisenhower Doctrine was invoked again in Syria, where pro-Communist forces were emerging in Syria's government. These forces included the Baath Socialist Party, which had ties with Egypt's President Nasser, and the Communist Party, which was linked to the Soviet Union. As a result of these growing influences, Syria began verbally attacking the United States and it expelled two American Embassy diplomats. Further aggravating the United States, Syria signed a major military and economic aid deal with the Soviet

Union and promoted a pro-Soviet general to head the Syrian army.

The United States saw these actions as indications that the Communists were taking over Syria's government. So did Syria's neighbors, Turkey, Iraq, and Jordan, who wanted to send their own troops to Syrian borders to intimidate Syria into ousting the Communists. President Eisenhower reacted by threatening to support Syria's neighbors if they chose to confront Syria, warning both the Soviet Union and Israel not to interfere, and sending the U.S. Air Force to the area. This, along with the appearance of Turkish troops on the Syrian border, helped to prevent a Communist takeover of Syria and marked another victory for Eisenhower's anti-Communist policy. However, Syria did not become a U.S. ally; instead, its government continued to be dominated by pro-Communist and radical forces, as events would soon reveal.

The U.S. Intervention in Lebanon

The most significant U.S. intervention under the Eisenhower Doctrine took place in Lebanon. In February 1958, as part of Egyptian president Nasser's Pan-Arabism, Syria and Egypt agreed to join into one country called the United Arab Republic. This development, however, was disturbing to some Arab states, such as Jordan, Saudi Arabia, and Lebanon. These countries feared that Pan-Arabists would overthrow their pro-Western governments.

In Lebanon, however, a large segment of its Muslim population was sympathetic to Pan-Arabism. They were also angry with their president, Camille Chamoun, for seeking close ties with the United States and violating the Lebanese constitution by securing a six-year term as president. In the spring of 1958 a coalition of Muslim and radical forces rebelled against Chamoun and seized control of Lebanon's capital, Beirut, as well as rural areas. Soon, they began receiving armed assistance from Syria, Egypt's main ally and a major supporter of Pan-Arabism. In May Chamoun appealed to the United States for help.

At first the United States was reluctant to send troops into Lebanon, fearing adverse reactions from other Arab countries in the Middle East. However, events in Iraq that summer soon changed U.S. opinion. In July 1958 a coup in Iraq replaced the British-installed monarchy with a pro-Nasser general, Abdul Karim Kassem. Kassem quickly aligned the new Iraqi government with the Pan-Arab United Arab Republic. To Eisenhower, this event signaled that Pan-Arabism might spread throughout the Middle East and could potentially set the stage for a massive Soviet move into the region. To prevent such a scenario, Eisenhower sent U.S. troops to Lebanon.

At the same time, Eisenhower sent his special emissary, Robert Murphy, to the area to find a peaceful solution to the crisis. Murphy arranged for a compromise candidate—someone acceptable to the United States, Nasser, and the majority of the Lebanese—to become president of Lebanon. The plan succeeded and U.S. troops were withdrawn in October 1958. The U.S.

Lebanese president Camille Chamoun addresses his people over the radio in 1958. Chamoun asked for U.S. help to quell anti-Western uprisings.

intervention left Lebanon, once controlled by Britain, under U.S. influence.

The American action in Lebanon was viewed by some U.S. policy makers as a successful application of the Eisenhower Doctrine; others said the United States had overstepped its limits. Under the doctrine, the president was only supposed to act to prevent "overt armed aggression from any nation controlled by International Communism."[14] However, in Lebanon there was only a threat from local Lebanese rebels, aided by Pan-Arabists from Syria, and so international communism was not a factor. Eisenhower supporters rejected this argument, saying that Nasser and the Pan-Arabists were controlled by the Soviet Union. However, as historian

Pan-Arabism

Pan-Arabism, also called Nasserism, was popularized by Gamal Abdel Nasser, who came to power in Egypt in 1952. President Nasser tried to unify the Arab nations of the Middle East in order to increase Arab political power and independence and resist British and American political control. For many Arabs, Pan-Arabism provided a positive message of hope and self-determination.

Pan-Arabists wanted to create a broad Pan-Arab coalition, and to this end, Syria and Egypt in 1958 formed the United Arab Republic. Nasser also tried to spread Pan-Arabism to other Middle Eastern countries, such as Lebanon, Yemen, Jordan, Saudi Arabia, and Iraq. Pan-Arabism succeeded in polarizing the Arab world into two groups—radical, anti-Western, Pan-Arabist countries (Egypt, Syria, Iraq, Yemen, and Algeria) and conservative, pro-Western countries (Saudi Arabia, Jordan, Kuwait, Libya, and Morocco) whose governments feared losing control to Arab nationalism. The United States, although at first supportive of the idea of Arab independence, later opposed Nasser's policies, especially after Nasser turned to the Soviet Union for military aid and support. Nasser's defeat by Israel in the Arab-Israeli War of 1967 and Nasser's death in 1970 marked the end of the pan-Arab movement.

George Lenczowski explains, "Nasser was neither a Communist nor a Soviet puppet. In fact, he curbed and suppressed native Communists both in Egypt and in Syria and, despite heavy dependence on Soviet arms and economic aid, jealously maintained his country's sovereignty."[15]

To Eisenhower it was clear that Nasser's Pan-Arabism was friendly with the Soviet Union and sought similar goals—the elimination of Western influence in the Middle East and the removal of pro-Western, conservative Arab governments. The success of Pan-Arabism, it was thought, might place U.S. economic interest in the hands of its enemies and end U.S. dominance in the Middle East. In Eisenhower's opinion, this was reason enough to do whatever was necessary to keep Pan-Arabism in check.

CHAPTER 3

Sowing the Seeds of Conflict—the Johnson and Nixon Years

By the 1960s the United States and the Soviet Union openly competed for influence in the Middle East, each supplying arms to their allies. Egyptian president Gamal Abdel Nasser increasingly turned to the Soviet Union for arms and support. Nasser's relationship with the Soviets, in turn, caused the United States to supply arms to Israel to counter Communist influence in the region. It has been rumored, but never confirmed by either nation, that the United States assisted Israel in developing nuclear weapons during this period. Thus, during the 1960s and 1970s, both the U.S. and the Soviet Union armed this increasingly volatile part of the world, sowing the seeds for future conflict.

The Six-Day War

The first of these tensions came when Israel and its Arab neighbors began ar-

guing over an Israeli plan to divert water from the Jordan River. Israel needed the increased water resources for its growing agriculture and industry. The Arab states opposed this project and began a project to divert the river into Syria and Jordan instead. However, the Israeli military attacked the Arab construction project and forced it to be abandoned. This, in turn, caused increasing friction on the Syrian-Israeli border, leading to sporadic gunfights between the Syrian and Israeli armies, as well as concern in other Arab states.

In early May 1967 Arab-Israeli tensions escalated even more when the Soviet Union informed Egypt that Israel had heavy troop concentrations on the Syrian-Israeli border and that Israel was planning to attack Syria. This information later proved to be false, but it set in motion a series of events that would have profound consequences for the Middle East. Acting on the Soviet tip, Nasser sent Egyptian troops to the Israeli border and once again closed the Gulf of Aqaba to Israeli ships.

Israel viewed the troop buildup and gulf closure as acts of aggression and decided to strike Egypt before it could attack Israel. Before embarking on this mission, however, Israel consulted with U.S. officials. The United States urged caution and warned Israel not to go to war, believing that Egypt did not really want war and would not attack. However, President Lyndon B. Johnson did not forcefully oppose Israeli war preparations. Indeed, on May 23 he authorized a secret shipment of weapons and military equipment to Israel, implicitly encouraging the Israelis.

Disregarding the weak U.S. warnings, Israel launched a surprise attack on June 5, 1967, destroying most of Egypt's air force. At the same time, Israel attacked Egyptian ground forces and again captured from Egypt the Sinai Peninsula and the Gaza Strip. Although the Arabs were well equipped, Israel's army and air force dramatically defeated Egyptian forces in just three days. Next, Israel attacked Egypt's military allies. It destroyed Jordan's air bases and seized the Jordanian-held territories of Jerusalem and the West Bank. Finally, Israel advanced into Syrian territory and captured the area known as the Golan Heights.

Resolution 242

Although the United Nations adopted Resolution 242 in 1967, it has never been fully implemented. Israel's security concerns and Arab nations' resulting unwillingness to make peace have prevented full application of the resolution, which orders Israel to withdraw from occupied territories and Arab nations to make peace with Israel. Arguments over the interpretations of the document have also prevented its enforcement. The full text of this controversial document can be found on the United Nations Web site.

The [UN] Security Council, expressing its continuing concern with the grave situation in the Middle East . . . requires the establishment of a just and lasting peace in the Middle East which should include the application of both the following principles:

(i) Withdrawal of Israel armed forces from territories occupied in the recent conflict;

(ii) Termination of all claims or states of belligerency and respect for and acknowledgment of the sovereignty, territorial integrity and political independence of every State in the area and their right to live in peace within secure and recognized boundaries free from threats or acts of force. . . .

[The UN Charter] affirms further the necessity . . . for achieving a just settlement of the refugee problem.

Israeli troops head for the Suez front as a truckload of stripped Egyptian prisoners of war leaves it. The war lasted only six days.

Just six days after the initial attack, the war ended with a cease-fire and a spectacular Israeli victory. In the lightning-fast fighting, Israel had captured multiple Arab territories—Gaza, the Sinai Peninsula, all of Jerusalem, the West Bank, and the Golan Heights. As professors Ian J. Bickerton and Carla L. Klausner explain, "[After the 1967 war] a new map of the Middle East came into being, with Israel three times larger than it was in 1949."[16] The war established Israel's military dominance in the Middle East. However, it also created more than three hundred thousand new Palestinian refugees and left the Arab world deeply humiliated, further heightening tensions between Arabs and Israelis.

Throughout the war the United States took various actions in support of Israel. For example, the United States opposed a UN proposal to order Israel to return to its prewar boundaries, thus supporting Israel's claim to the additional territories as lands conquered during war. Also, in a highly controversial incident on June 8 involving an Israeli attack on an American intelligence-gathering ship, the USS *Liberty*, President Johnson accepted Israeli claims that the attack was an error, despite indications to the contrary. Many believe that Israel deliberately destroyed the *Liberty* because, as

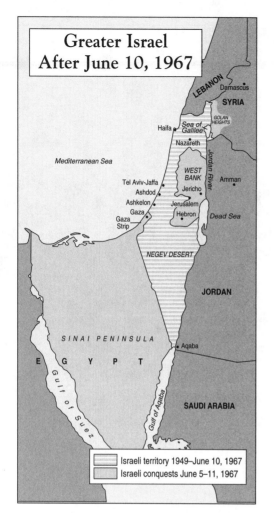

Greater Israel After June 10, 1967

LEBANON
Damascus
SYRIA
GOLAN HEIGHTS
Haifa
Sea of Galilee
Nazareth
Mediterranean Sea
Jordan River
WEST BANK
Amman
Tel Aviv-Jaffa
Ashdod
Jericho
Ashkelon
Jerusalem
Gaza
Hebron
Dead Sea
Gaza Strip
NEGEV DESERT
JORDAN
SINAI PENINSULA
Aqaba
E G Y P T
Gulf of Suez
Gulf of Aqaba
SAUDI ARABIA

Israeli territory 1949–June 10, 1967
Israeli conquests June 5–11, 1967

historian George Lenczowski writes, "Israel clearly did not want the U.S. government to know too much about its war operations and orders."[17]

Finally, when Israel was poised to attack Damascus (the capital of Syria), and the Soviets threatened to intervene, the United States sent the U.S. Navy's Sixth Fleet to the area in support of Israel until it was able to persuade Israel to cease its military actions. In each of these instances, America's support for Israel further divided it from the Arab nations.

Growing Arab Anger at U.S. Pro-Israel policies

The American backing of Israel during the Six-Day War, along with its failure to demand that Israel return the Arab territories it had taken, was hugely frustrating to the defeated Arabs, especially Palestinians who hoped for an independent Palestinian state. Arab countries, bitter and humiliated, met at an Arab League summit in September 1967 and agreed there would be "no negotiations, no recognition and no peace with Israel."[18] The Arab League demanded that the United Nations order Israel to withdraw from the territories occupied during the war.

Instead, U.S. diplomats succeeded in getting the United Nations to adopt Resolution 242, a land-for-peace compromise, which stated that Israel should withdraw from territories occupied in the war and that Arabs, in return, should recognize Israel and its right to live in peace.

From this point on, America became widely perceived in the Arab world as a close ally of Israel that pursued pro-Israel and anti-Arab policies. As a result, six Arab states—Egypt, Syria, Iraq, Yemen, Algeria, and Sudan—ended diplomatic relations with the United States and aligned themselves with the Soviet Union. In this way, another result of the 1967 war was increased Cold War polarity.

Over the next several years, under the policies of President Richard Nixon, the United States increasingly became even more allied with Israel. The two countries deepened their relationship into a strategic partnership in which Israel became a proxy (or deputy) for American power in the Middle East and a key to thwarting Soviet influence in the area. As a result, U.S. aid to Israel, which had averaged about $63 million per year before the Six-Day War, sharply increased after the war. Much of this aid was for Israel's military. As analyst Sheldon L. Richman explains, "From 1966 through 1970 . . . [U.S. aid to Israel] jumped to $102 million [annually],

The Israeli Attack on the USS *Liberty*

During the Arab-Israeli War of 1967, Israeli forces attacked an American intelligence-gathering ship, the USS *Liberty*, stationed in the Mediterranean Sea. The United States had sent the *Liberty* to the area to collect information about the war. On June 8, 1967, *Liberty* moved close to the shores of Egypt but still remained in international waters. At 4:05 P.M. that day, after first being viewed by several Israeli airplanes, the *Liberty* was attacked by Israeli jets and torpedo boats. When life rafts were lowered to allow the American sailors on the *Liberty* to escape, the Israelis also fired on them. As a result of the attack, 34 Americans were killed and 171 wounded.

Israel claimed the attack was an error, even though the ship is said to have prominently displayed an American flag and U.S. Navy identification marks that were clearly visible from the air. U.S. president Lyndon Johnson quickly accepted

the Israeli explanation without challenge. Later, a naval court of inquiry was convened and the crew of the *Liberty* was ordered not to say anything about the attack. To many, this suggests a government cover-up of the incident. Many also believe that Israel deliberately attacked the *Liberty* to prevent the United States from learning about its war plans, especially its secret plan for attacking Syria. American knowledge of this plan might have enabled it to prevent Israel from conquering the Golan Heights, which had been controlled by Syria until the Israeli attack.

The USS Liberty *shows damage from the Israeli air attack in 1967.*

and the share of military loans climbed to 47 percent."[19] Thereafter, U.S. military support for Israel grew astronomically, reaching approximately $1.8 billion per year by the late 1990s. The Soviets, in turn, increased their economic and military aid to Arab states. In this way, the Six-Day War continued an escalating arms race in the Middle East.

Israel as America's Proxy

Events occurring in Jordan in 1970 helped cement the close American-Israeli relationship. Jordan during this period became the headquarters for Palestinian militant groups, such as the Palestine Liberation Organization (PLO). The PLO used violence and terrorism to fight for the establishment of an independant Palestinian state. In one of

In 1970 PLO hijackers blew up this and three other airliners in Jordan. The crisis revealed the firm alliance between America and Israel.

these terrorist acts, in September 1970, a group associated with the PLO hijacked four civilian airliners from various countries, brought them to Jordan, and blew them up. Jordan's government was incensed by this incident and tried to evict the PLO from the country, sparking what amounted to a civil war in Jordan. Syria, an enemy of Jordan's pro-Western government, soon sent tanks into Jordan to protect the PLO.

The crisis in Jordan was viewed by U.S. policy makers as a sign of Soviet intervention in the region, because the Soviets were supporters of Syria. Seeking to protect its allies, Jordan and Israel, the United States warned Syria to stop its invasion. It also authorized Israel to make air strikes on Syrian forces. In the end, however, neither Israeli nor U.S. military action was necessary. Jordan's air force attacked the Syrian tanks, forcing Syria to withdraw. The PLO was ousted from Jordan and moved its headquarters to Lebanon.

This incident illustrated that America relied on Israel to act as its proxy, or substitute, in Middle East disputes. In other words, U.S. interests could be protected without having to send American troops into volatile areas in the Middle East and without directly confronting the Soviets. The fact that the United States was depending on Israel, a longtime enemy of Arabs, to intervene in what was essentially an Arab versus Arab conflict made clear to Arabs that the United States was working hand in hand with Israel. It also left the United States indebted to Israel. In-

deed, after the Jordan incident, President Nixon sent a note to Israeli prime minister Yitzhak Rabin, thanking him and stating, "The United States is fortunate in having an ally like Israel in the Middle East. These events will be taken into account in all future developments."[20] Ever since, American aid to Israel has flowed uninterrupted, and Israel has been seen as America's strongest ally in the Middle East.

The 1973 Yom Kippur War— Confronting the Soviets

The United States became involved in yet another Arab-Israeli battle in 1973—one that almost brought it into a direct nuclear confrontation with the Soviets. The conflict began in 1970 after Egyptian president Gamal Abdel Nasser's unexpected death. Egypt's new president, Anwar Sadat, began a campaign to regain Arab pride and convince Israel to withdraw from some of the territories it seized during the Six-Day War. Sadat first tried diplomacy, offering to reopen the Suez Canal to Israeli ships. He also offered a cease-fire and a peace agreement with Israel if it would withdraw from parts of the Sinai Peninsula. When Israel still refused to give up territory, Sadat threatened to regain Egypt's lost lands by force.

On October 6, 1973, Egyptian forces, together with troops from its ally Syria, launched a surprise attack on Israel on Yom Kippur, Judaism's most somber holiday. The war, which came to be known in Israel as the Yom Kippur War, resulted in very heavy fighting. The Egyptians inflicted serious damage on Israel while Syria attacked Israeli positions in the Golan Heights. At the outbreak of war, the United States sent a massive airlift of arms, military supplies, and aid to Israel. As historian George Lenczowski notes, "All in all, 550 American missions to Israel carried out the task of supply and resupply,"[21] an operation of great magnitude. In addition, the United States sent Israel $2.2 billion in emergency aid.

In response, the Organization of Petroleum Exporting Countries (OPEC), which included Saudi Arabia, a U.S. ally, in October 1973, stopped delivering all Middle East oil to America. This oil embargo damaged the world economy and caused a worldwide recession (an economic downturn). This was the first time in history that Arab countries succeeded in using oil as a weapon.

The Yom Kippur War soon brought the United States close to a nuclear standoff with the Soviets. At the same time as the United States was arming Israel, the Soviets were arming Egypt. In late October, when Israel ignored a UN cease-fire order and advanced toward Egypt, the Soviets proposed a joint U.S.-Soviet military intervention to end the fighting. If the United States declined to help, the Soviets warned that they would consider taking action alone to halt Israel's advance. Although later it was learned that the Soviets sincerely wanted cooperation rather than confrontation, the United States at the time viewed the Soviet threat as aggressive and put all its military forces, including nuclear forces, on alert. This reaction placed the superpowers in a

tense and dangerous nuclear standoff and threatened the process of détente, an effort by the United States and the Soviet Union in the 1970s to relax Cold War tensions.

Ultimately, however, the Soviets backed down and did not send troops to Egypt. The war ended with a cease-fire negotiated by the United States and the Soviet Union. It was approved by the United Nations in Resolution 338, which called on the parties to begin direct peace negotiations. In the end, Israel was badly shaken by the Arab attack, because the war showed that Israel was not invincible as it had seemed after its 1967 victory. Over the next couple of years, Israel again returned Egyptian and Syrian lands it had seized during the Six-Day War. In return, Egypt again opened the Suez Canal for Israeli ships. This successful end to the Egypt-Israel dispute, in turn, ended the Arab oil embargo.

In retrospect, America's support for Israel during the Yom Kippur War was very costly and destabilizing. Not only did the war and its aftermath cost American taxpayers billions in additional military and other aid to Israel, the oil embargo had plunged the United States into a deep recession accompanied by high unemployment. Furthermore, the war had increased Arab anger against America and exposed the country to a nuclear brush with the Soviets. As analyst Sheldon L. Richman explains, "Total support of Israel did not create stability; on the contrary, it further alienated the Arabs, pushed several Arab states closer to the Soviet Union, upset

The 1973 Oil Embargo

During the Yom Kippur War between Israel and Egypt, the Organization of Petroleum Exporting Countries (OPEC) imposed an embargo on oil exports to the United States. The embargo, announced on October 17, 1973, prohibited the export of oil to the United States and imposed price increase of as much as 70 percent on American's Western European allies. Overnight, the price of oil in Europe went from $3 per barrel to $5.11 per barrel. Prices rose as high as $11.65 per barrel a few months later.

The oil embargo caused a worldwide recession that was felt throughout the world. In the United States, long lines of cars waited to fill up at gas stations. The demand for gas was so high and the supply was so low that rationing systems were devised in some states to dole out gas to everyone. Indeed, red flags were a common sight at some gas stations, indicating they were completely out of fuel. In addition, the embargo resulted in the loss of five hundred thousand jobs and from $10 billion to $20 billion in gross national product, a measurement of economic output.

For the Arabs, the embargo worked to pressure the United States to help resolve the Israel-Egypt conflict. It was ended on March 18, 1974, when Israel agreed to return certain Syrian and Egyptian lands it had seized during the war to its Egyptian and Syrian neighbors.

U.S. motorists rush to fill their gas tanks during the 1973 Arab oil embargo.

An Israeli soldier accompanies Egyptian POWs during the 1973 Yom Kippur War. The war brought America and the Soviet Union to a nuclear standoff.

U.S.-Soviet détente, and loaded the OPEC oil weapon."[22]

Nixon's Twin Pillars Policy

The United States during this period also sought to expand its Middle East alliances beyond Israel. For example, President Nixon designated two Arab nations—Iran and Saudi Arabia—as U.S. allies and defenders in the Middle East. This policy became known as Nixon's Twin Pillars policy.

The policy originated in 1968, when Britain announced it intended to with-draw its military forces from the Persian Gulf area, which includes Iran, Iraq, Saudi Arabia, and numerous smaller and weaker countries such as Kuwait, Bahrain, Qatar, the United Arab Emirates, and Oman. These Persian Gulf countries contain some of the world's largest oil reserves, which are highly valuable to developed countries whose economies demand large amounts of fuel. The United States feared that the power vacuum after Britain's pullout would lead to Soviet efforts to dominate such prized territory. However, because

America was unable to undertake new military commitments due to its entanglement in the Vietnam War, it urged the Western-leaning countries of Iran and Saudi Arabia to assume the responsibility for defense of the gulf.

As part of this policy, the United States agreed to sell technologically advanced weapons to Iran. In exchange, Iran agreed to protect U.S. oil interests in the region. Indeed, Nixon, in a visit with the shah of Iran in May 1972, not only agreed to provide Iran with all the weapons it was requesting at that time, he also ordered that "in the future Iran-ian requests should not be second-guessed,"[23] thus giving Iran unprecedented access to coveted U.S. weapons systems.

For the rest of the decade, therefore, Iran became a major recipient of U.S. arms and military aid. In this way, Iran, like Israel, became an anti-Communist proxy that could exercise military power on behalf of the United States. In the mid-1970s, for example, as part of the U.S. plan to keep the Communists out of the Persian Gulf, Iran sent forces to Oman to prevent it from being taken over by Communist rebels there. Many

President Richard Nixon (center) greets the shah of Iran in 1969. Nixon created alliances with Iran and Saudi Arabia to protect U.S. interests.

Iranians and much of the Arab world, however, viewed this policy as U.S. domination of Iran. These anti-American tensions, by the end of the 1970s, would result in an explosive crash of the Iranian pillar of U.S. defense.

The Saudi Arabia pillar, unlike Iran, was never very strong. Saudi Arabia's participation in the 1973 oil embargo against the United States made its loyalty questionable, as did the country's financial support of the PLO. In spite of this, the United States provided the Saudis with advanced weaponry. As with Iran, the United States had chosen to overlook Saudi Arabia's repression of its citizens. This policy was seen by many in the Arab world as hypocritical, given that America often touted itself as a defender of freedom and democracy. The Twin Pillars policy, therefore, was largely a failure and, like many other U.S. Middle East policies during this period, only served to plant the seeds for Arab and Islamic distrust of America.

CHAPTER 4

Fallout from U.S. Policies— the Beginning of Anti-U.S. Terrorism

I n the late 1970s and 1980s U.S. Middle East policies for the first time began to make Americans vulnerable to Arab and Islamic terrorist attacks. First, the United States experienced a backlash from its pro-Israel policies and emerged as an enemy of much of the Arab and Muslim world. Second, America's policies in Iran helped incite an Islamic revolution and an American hostage crisis, decisively ending the U.S. alliance with that country. Finally, America's continuing anti-Communist policy in the region armed a new group of Islamic fundamentalists in Afghanistan who would eventually turn their violence upon America. These events began to reveal the flaws in previous U.S. Middle East policies.

The U.S. Role in the 1978 Camp David Accords

One of the first concrete events that began to undo America's image in the Arab world was the Camp David Accords, an attempt to secure peace between the Israelis and Arabs. To this end, President Jimmy Carter in 1978 for the first time used personal presidential diplomacy to push for agreement between the two sides. Carter's position on Israel was clear. As he explained in 1977, "We have a special relationship with Israel. It's absolutely crucial that no one in our country or around the world ever doubt that our number-one commitment in the Middle East is to protect the right of Israel to exist, to exist permanently, and to exist in peace."[24]

(Left to right) Israel's Prime Minister Menachem Begin, President Jimmy Carter, and Egypt's President Anwar Sadat pose at Camp David, where they produced a peace agreement.

Carter's peace efforts were inspired by a bold peace gesture from Egyptian president Anwar Sadat in 1977. Sadat offered to personally fly to Israel to discuss peace in the first-ever face-to-face negotiations between Arabs and Israelis. Sadat wanted to make a peace deal with Israel because Egypt's hostilities with Israel had simply become too expensive; peace would allow Sadat to reduce military expenditures and focus on economic rebuilding in his country. In a surprising response to Sadat's move, Israeli prime minister Menachem Begin, known as a hard-liner politician, invited Sadat to travel to Israel and address the Israeli parliament, called the Knesset. In the dramatic speech, Sadat presented his peace plan and told Israelis that Egypt wanted to live with Israel in a permanent peace.

Following Sadat's visit to Israel, the two sides began U.S.-chaperoned peace negotiations. In September 1978, President Carter invited Begin and Sadat to his presidential retreat in Camp David, Maryland. The meeting produced two accords, or agreements, which later came to be known as the Camp David Accords. Under these agreements, Israel was to allow a self-governing, elected Palestinian authority to operate in the West Bank and Gaza, two of the areas seized from Arabs by Israel in 1967. In addition, the accords required Israel to withdraw from all of Sinai, an Egyptian territory seized by Israel. In exchange, Egypt agreed to establish peaceful relations with Israel and guarantee Israel's unrestricted access to the Suez Canal. On March 26, 1979, Sadat and Begin signed an Egyptian-Israeli peace treaty that is still in effect today. The Camp David Accords thus provided the first peace between Israel and an Arab state.

In America, the peace accords were hailed as a triumph for peace in the Middle East. President Carter's ultimate goal was to broker a comprehensive Arab-Israeli peace, which would result in greater Middle East stability. However, Arab reactions to the accords were overwhelmingly negative.

To the Arab world, Egypt, the most powerful Arab country, had betrayed common Arab goals of forcing Israel to withdraw from all Arab territories and creating an independent Palestinian state. Furthermore, Arabs felt Egypt had traded these goals for a separate peace with Israel without even consulting them. As the realities of the Camp David plan emerged, Palestinians and other Arabs became even angrier. Israel made it clear that it intended to limit the amount of authority granted to the Palestinians and rejected any idea that the accords would lead to an Israeli withdrawal from the West Bank and Gaza. As a result, the Arab League, led by Arab states such as Syria, Iraq, Al-geria, Libya, and South Yemen imposed political and economic sanctions against Egypt and suspended it from the league. For its role in the accords, America, too, was further discredited in the Arab and Islamic world.

Israel Invades Lebanon

Support for Israel continued under America's next president, Ronald Reagan, who considered Israel key to opposing communism in the Middle East. Reagan once explained, for example, that Israel is "perhaps the only remaining strategic asset in the region on which the United States can truly rely . . . her facilities and air fields could provide a secure point of access if required in . . . [an] emergency."[25] As a result, the United States during Reagan's presidency made sure that Israel maintained military superiority over all other Middle Eastern countries by dramatically increasing U.S. aid. Indeed, over the eight years of the Reagan presidency, the United States gave more than $27 billion to Israel—more than all the aid that had been provided to Israel until that time.

Israel soon employed its enhanced military might. In 1982, under the leadership of Prime Minister Menachem Begin and Defense Minister Ariel Sharon, Israel invaded the neighboring country of Lebanon with a massive force that eventually totaled eighty thousand men and 1,240 tanks. The invasion was an effort to destroy the main Palestinian militant group, the PLO, which was using Lebanon, as it had Jordan, as a base for striking at Israel. Sharon was also concerned about Syrian missiles located in Lebanon, which could be used to hit Israeli targets.

Suspecting that both the PLO and Lebanon were receiving support from the Soviet Union, the United States supported the invasion plan as a way to weaken pro-Soviet forces in the Middle East. Indeed, as analyst Avi Shlaim notes, at a meeting in May 1981, just before the Israeli invasion, "[U.S. secretary of state Alexander] Haig indicated that the United States would not oppose a limited Israeli military operation in Lebanon, provided it could be justified. [As a result,] Sharon concluded that he had received a green light."[26]

Once begun, however, the Israeli invasion of Lebanon became highly controversial. While Israel claimed its goal was to clear the PLO from southern Lebanon and create a twenty-five-mile wide security zone on the Lebanese side of the border, Israeli defense minister Sharon carried out a much more aggressive campaign. Israeli forces advanced past the twenty-five mile mark and attacked Beirut, Lebanon's capital city, killing thousands of Lebanese and Palestinian civilians and creating tens of thousands of refugees. Moreover, the invasion became an occupation when Israel refused to leave until the PLO was ousted from Lebanese territory.

The most controversial portion of the war occurred on September 14, 1982, when anti-PLO Lebanese leader Bashir Gemayel was assassinated by supporters of the PLO. After the assassination, Israeli troops permitted followers of Gemayel to enter the Palestinian refugee camps Sabra and Shatilla to seek revenge. A brutal massacre ensued, and between six and eight hundred Palestinians—men, women, and children—were killed.

Growing U.S. Support for Israel

Under U.S. president Ronald Reagan's administration, support for Israel grew to unprecedented levels. U.S. government military and economic aid to Israel, which for thirty-nine years had averaged less than $1 billion per year, by 1986 had more than tripled to $3 billion a year. The United States during this period looked the other way when Israel took actions that many in the international community condemned as aggressive and destabilizing for the Middle East. For example, in 1981 Israel bombed and destroyed a nuclear reactor in Iraq, fearful that Iraq might use nuclear power for offensive purposes against Israel. The United States, in response, temporarily delayed the shipment of fighter jets to Israel, but the incident did not affect the U.S.-Israeli relationship in the long run. That same year, Israel formally annexed (or made part of Israel) the Golan Heights, a territory whose status had not been officially resolved, previously under Syria's control but occupied by Israel during the 1967 war. Once again, the United States lightly punished Israel by suspending a strategic accord but took no further action.

U.S.-backed Israeli forces invade Lebanon in 1982. Israel sought to destroy PLO and Syrian threats there, while America wanted to blunt Soviet influence.

The murders were described as "butchery" by Israeli journalists Ze-ev Schiff and Ehud Ya-ari: "In addition to the wholesale slaughter of families, the [Gemayel supporters] indulged in such sadistic horrors as hanging live grenades around their victims' necks. In one particularly vicious act of barbarity, an infant was trampled to death by a man wearing spiked shoes. The entire . . . action in Sabra and Shatilla seemed to be directed against civilians."[27] Although Israeli soldiers did not directly participate in the slaughter, they allowed it to happen.

U.S. Support for Israel Makes America a Terror Target

The invasion of Lebanon brought worldwide condemnation of Israel. The UN Security Council unanimously demanded an immediate cease-fire and sought to condemn Israel's actions. However, the United States used its veto power to block enforcement of the UN measure. Instead, President Reagan negotiated for the departure of the PLO from Lebanon, a result sought by Israel. In addition, the United States sent a naval armada to the area, and against

Corpses litter the street of a Palestinian refugee camp in Beirut after the Sabra and Shatilla massacres. The atrocities turned world opinion against Israel.

the advice of many in Congress and other U.S. policy makers, sent eighteen hundred American soldiers into Lebanon as part of a multinational peacekeeping force. By August 1982 the evacuation of Palestinian fighters was begun, and the United States promised to protect Palestinian civilians left in Lebanon. Israel left Beirut in May 1983 but maintained troops in southern Lebanon until 2000 to provide a security buffer.

Israel's actions were criticized even in Israel, where news of the Sabra and Shatilla massacres led to massive demonstrations against Israel's war in Lebanon and to a new phenomenon of Israeli soldiers becoming conscientious objectors and refusing to serve in the army. As analyst Avi Shlaim notes, Israel was revealed "not as a bastion of stability but a source of regional turmoil and violence."[28]

Because of America's uncritical support for Israel throughout the Lebanon invasion, Arabs concluded that the United States was a willing partner in Israel's crimes and had allowed the Sabra and Shatilla incident to occur, in spite of its promise to protect Palestinians in Lebanon. Furthermore, Arabs claimed that U.S. peacekeeping forces in Lebanon took sides, demonstrating that America could not be trusted as an impartial peacemaker or mediator in the conflict. As a result, America's reputation in the Arab world dropped to a new low.

The degree of Arab anger at America soon became evident, as Arab terrorists began targeting U.S. soldiers and diplomats stationed in Lebanon. On April 18, 1983, an Arab Islamic terrorist group called Islamic Jihad set off a bomb at the U.S. embassy in Beirut,

killing forty-six and injuring close to one hundred. A few months later, on October 23, a truck driven by a Muslim suicide bomber and loaded with twenty-five hundred pounds of TNT explosives drove into the U.S. Marine headquarters in Beirut. In the huge explosion, 265 U.S. Marines were killed. Also, in December 1983, an Iranian militant group, Dawa (the Call), launched a truck bomb attack on U.S. and French embassies in Kuwait. These terrorist attacks on U.S. targets shocked America, because the United States had experienced few incidents of terrorism in the past. Soon, in February 1984, the United States decided to leave Lebanon.

America had paid dearly for its ties with Israel. Its reputation was damaged, regional security was decreased, and

The Islamic Revolution

After the Islamic revolution, a conservative religious way of life was adopted in Iran. Because the leaders of the revolution strictly interpreted Islamic laws, they banned such things as music and alcohol. They also rejected anything that was Western to show their distaste for the United States, which they believed had wrongly meddled in their country. Robin Wright, author of The Last Great Revolution: Turmoil and Transformation in Iran, *explains some of the changes that took place:*

Cultural outlets [such as discos or cafés] were forcibly closed. University life was suspended while curriculum was reviewed [to erase any material that was deemed offensive to Islam]. Bars and nightclubs had their liquor stocks destroyed before being boarded up. Religious vigilantes monitored morality in each neighborhood. Streets were often empty at night, because pedestrians and drivers wanted to avoid searches at impromptu checkpoints set up by the new Revolutionary Guards.

Even fashion changed. Women were forced [to put on] chadors and hejab, the generic term for a variety of body covers. Many simply retreated to their homes. To show loyalty [to the revolution], men grew beards or a permanent three-day stubble. Ties, the epitome of Western style, became taboo.

U.S. Marines carry a wounded comrade from their bombed Beirut headquarters in 1983. Islamic terrorists killed 265 marines in the attack.

anti-American terrorism had cost hundreds of lives. For many, the Lebanese campaign demonstrated the folly of American pro-Israel policies. As commentator Avi Shlaim states, "More than any other episode, the Lebanon war exposed the bankruptcy of . . . the Israel-first approach as a framework for formulating American policy toward the Middle East."[29]

The Collapse of the Iran Pillar

American policy in the Middle East further backfired during this period when it lost one of its strongest allies in the region: Iran. The United States had long supported the shah of Iran, despite the fact that opposition to his rule had been brewing for a long time among Iranians. Although certain programs instituted under the shah had helped to modernize Iran and bring it wealth, the shah's rule was characterized by torture and other human rights violations. Moreover, the shah outlawed many forms of religious expression at a time when Iranians were actively embracing Shiism, the sect of Islam widely practiced in Iran. Indeed, many in Iran wanted an Islamic government to replace the secular government of the shah, which was viewed as favoring Western values over those of Islam. Although the United States had begun to criticize the shah's policies, it did not suspect the depths of Iranian frustration and anger with the government. In January 1979, just a month after President Carter praised Iran as an "island of stability" in the Middle East, the United States was shocked by an Islamic revolution that overthrew the shah's regime.

In 1979 the Ayatollah Ruhollah Khomeini ousted the U.S.-backed regime in Iran and set up an Islamic government, ending Iran's alliance with America.

The revolution was led by religious leader Ayatollah Ruhollah Khomeini. Khomeini was beloved by Iranians; his outspoken views on the shah and America, along with his dedication to Islam, earned him great respect in the eyes of nearly all Iranians. Ultimately, the ayatollah encouraged Iranians to rebel against the shah, who was forced to leave the country. Khomeini set up a revolutionary Islamic government which was ardently anti-American—so much so that American citizens in Iran were no longer safe.

A crisis arose in November 1979, when the shah was admitted to the United States to seek medical care. Iranians interpreted this event as part of a plot by the United States to return the shah to power, and on November 4, a group of militant Iranian students assaulted the U.S. Embassy in Iran and took sixty-six Americans hostage. In the months that followed, the female and black hostages were released, but the remaining white male hostages were subjected to physical and psychological torture, much of it broadcast on worldwide television to humiliate America and its government officials.

The United States, under President Carter, first responded to the hostage crisis with diplomacy, and when that failed, with force. In April 1980 helicopters raced toward Iran on a covert rescue mission; the mission was aborted, however, when one of the helicopters was accidentally destroyed. The hostage crisis was not resolved until almost a year later, when the Ayatollah Khome-ini decided to pursue serious negotiations. After 444 days of captivity, fifty-two U.S. hostages finally walked free in January 1981.

The Beginning of Anti-American Terror

In Iran, America experienced the results of its decades-long support of the shah. Indeed, the Islamic revolution and hostage crisis decisively ended the long period of friendly U.S.-Iranian relations. With one blow, the events of 1979–1980 eliminated one of America's strongest Middle East allies, destroyed a large part of the U.S. plan for defending the Middle East, and left Israel as the only Middle Eastern state firmly allied with the United States.

The Iranian revolution also fueled and gave direction to the growing Islamic fundamentalist movement in the Middle East. This movement was comprised of Muslim extremists who wanted to install Islamic religious rule in countries throughout the Middle East. The goal of these Islamic fundamentalists was to protect the Arab world and Islam's cultural heritage from Western influences. They perceived the United States, Israel, and the various pro-Western Arab governments as their enemies and evils that must be resisted. The Islamic Revolution in Iran was seen by fundamentalists all over the Middle East as a great achievement and thus a model for revolution. Khomeini, a figurehead for this movement, called on Muslims to confront and attack the United States, which he called the "Great Satan."

In addition, the events in Iran made America look weak and thus spawned anti-American terrorism. Until the hostage crisis, America was seen by most around the world as a giant, too powerful to become the target of small groups of terrorists. The kidnapping of the American hostages in Iran, however, was a brash act of anti-American terrorism that directly targeted the United States. Worse, the drama unfolded slowly, over a period of months, and was publicized around the world. In this way, the hostage crisis revealed for

The Libyan Terrorist Threat

During the 1980s the United States experienced a number of terrorist attacks on its citizens and institutions around the world. One perpetrator of these attacks was Muammar Qaddafi, who became the ruler of Libya in a military coup in 1969. In the 1980s Qaddafi became one of the worlds most well-known anti-West terrorists. He supported Arab and Palestinian causes and condemned U.S. and Western policies which he felt wronged Arabs. In what would become Qaddafi's most infamous terrorist act, in September 1988 Libyan operatives blew up a Pan American airplane over Lockerbie, Scotland, killing 280 people. An investigation conducted by the United States and Britain concluded that two Libyan suspects that were linked to Libya's government were responsible for the bombing—Abdelbaset Ali Mohmed al-Megrahi and Al Amin Khalifa Fhimah.

In 1992 the United Nations imposed economic sanctions on Libya for its refusal to turn over the Lockerbie suspects; these sanctions effectively limited Qaddafi's ability to export terror. Finally, in 1999, Libya agreed to hand over al-Megrahi and Fhimah, allowing a suspension of the sanctions against Libya. The sanctions were completely lifted in 2003 after Libya agreed to pay compensation to families of the victims. These actions have caused some people to look at Qaddafi more favorably, though others still regard him with suspicion.

Libyan leader Muammar Qaddafi was a major source of anti-U.S. terrorism during the 1980s.

the first time the vulnerability of the United States to terrorist tactics. As historian David W. Lesch explains, "The Iranian revolution introduced the United States to a new era and a heightened level of anti-Americanism and political extremism. The psychological barriers and the taboo of striking directly at America seemed to have been lifted, inaugurating a period of Middle East terrorist activity that be- came inexorably linked with Middle East politics."[30]

The Iran-Iraq War and the U.S. Arming of Iraq

The Iranian revolution had yet another side effect; it led to a prolonged war between Iran and Iraq. During this conflict the United States switched its support from Iran to Iraq. In fact, it was during the Iran-Iraq War that the

Iraqi soldiers engage the enemy during the eight-year-long Iran-Iraq War. The United States backed Iraq against Iran, a former U.S. ally.

United States first began providing military support for Iraqi dictator Saddam Hussein.

The Islamic revolution in Iran was threatening to many Persian Gulf nations. Pro-Western governments in these countries were also contending with Islamic revolutionaries who were trying to take over their regimes. Indeed, Iran's Khomeini openly encouraged revolution in neighboring Iraq, de-

claring in April 1980, "The people and army of Iraq must turn their backs on [Saddam Hussein's government] and overthrow it."[31] Iraqi president Saddam Hussein responded by going to war with Iran. After numerous border skirmishes between the two countries, Iraq attacked Iran on September 22, 1980, beginning a long eight-year war.

Over the course of the war the United States (along with other nations such as Britain, France, and Russia) provided billions of dollars of military support and surveillance information to Iraq. This included materials to help Iraq develop chemical and biological weapons. The Iran-Iraq War finally ended with a UN-sponsored cease-fire and resolution accepted in 1988. Iraq emerged from the war crippled economically, but with a strong military. The war, therefore, and U.S. support, strengthened the regime of Saddam Hussein and turned Iraq into a formidable military power. As Mideast expert

Con Coughlin reports, "By 1988, Iraq had developed the fourth largest army in the world."[32] This arming of Saddam Hussein, however, was shortsighted; a few years later, Saddam would turn his newfound military strength against his neighbors, creating yet another Middle East crisis.

The Soviet Invasion of Afghanistan

While the Islamic Revolution in Iran was under way, another event in 1979 that had far-reaching consequences for America occurred when the Soviet Union invaded Afghanistan. The U.S. response was to support Afghan freedom fighters against the Soviets—yet another policy that later backfired and produced a wave of anti-American terrorism.

The trouble in Afghanistan began with a coup in 1973 that put Prince Sardar Mohammad Daud, a Soviet supporter, into power. After he became Afghanistan's ruler, however, Daud acted more independently, trying to steer a course that would not align Afghanistan with either the Soviets or the United States. Daud's policies displeased both the Soviets and pro-Soviet groups within Afghanistan, and he was overthrown in 1978. A Communist-style government was then formed, led by Noor Mohammad Taraki, which was closely monitored by about three thousand Soviet advisers. The new government quickly imposed Communist reforms, including land reforms which undermined the authority of tribal leaders. The new policies also replaced many Islamic traditions, which upset many religious Afghans.

These Communist reforms inspired disorganized groups of Afghan fighters to try to overthrow the Taraki regime. They became known as the mujahideen (meaning warriors for the faith), and they soon began a jihad, or holy war, against the Communist government. The mujahideen succeeded in taking control of large parts of the Afghan countryside, and by March 1979 they had even taken control of Herat, Afghanistan's second-largest city. Taraki's army tried to suppress the rebellion, leading to a full-scale civil war.

To regain control in Afghanistan, the Soviets conducted a massive military invasion on December 27, 1979. Over eighty thousand Soviet troops descended into the country, occupying major cities and highways. The Soviets took such measures because they feared that if an independent government came to power in Afghanistan, it might align itself with Iran or possibly even the United States, giving large foreign powers influence close to Soviet borders.

The U.S. Role in Afghanistan

The United States reacted strongly to this turn of events. U.S. policy makers saw that the Soviet Union was trying to establish dominance in Afghanistan and predicted that it would then move to the Persian Gulf. Under a policy that became known as the Carter Doctrine, the United States therefore warned the Soviets against any further aggression and pledged to defend the gulf from Soviet moves. President Carter made this declaration in his State of the Union address on January 23, 1980, stating, "An attempt by any outside force to gain control of the Persian Gulf region will be regarded as an assault on the vital interests of the United States [and] will be repelled by any means necessary, including military force."[33] The United States also formed a special military command called the Rapid Deployment Force to be ready to fight the Soviets if they moved into the Persian Gulf. For the United States, the Soviet invasion of Afghanistan had revived the Cold War.

However, a direct war in Afghanistan between two superpowers that both had nuclear weapons would be too risky. Instead, President Carter, and America's next president, Ronald Reagan, provided covert (that is secret) support for the Islamic mujahideen fighters. Together, the Central Intelligence Agency (CIA) and Saudi Arabia's intelligence service channeled about $6 billion in arms to the Afghan resistance movement, including sophisticated weapons such as Stinger antiaircraft missiles. Another U.S. ally, Pakistan, helped transfer the U.S. aid to the mujahideen. The United States also encouraged

Afghan mujahideen resist Soviet invaders in 1980. Ironically, U.S. support for the Afghans led to the rise of terrorist leader Osama bin Laden.

other Muslim countries to support the Afghan freedom fighters, and soon Muslim volunteers arrived in Afghanistan from all over the world. Indeed, one of these Muslim fighters was Osama bin Laden, a wealthy Saudi who became invested in the Afghan cause. Faced with this broad support for the Afghans, and a mountainous terrain that made it nearly impossible for Soviet troops to control the countryside, the Soviets withdrew from the country by 1989.

Ironically, the Afghanistan crisis ultimately marked the end of the Cold War, as the costs of the war destroyed the Soviet economy and led to the collapse of the Soviet Union in 1991. However, American support for the mujahideen eventually bore bitter fruit for the United States. After the Soviet withdrawal, Afghanistan was left both physically devastated by the war and without any clear leadership. Under these conditions, various tribes fought for power in a continuing civil war. Finally, a fundamentalist Muslim group, called the Taliban, restored order and gained control of Afghanistan. The Taliban government, as professor David W. Lesch describes, became "an outpost of Islamic extremism and a lightning rod of Muslim discontent with the West, particularly with [the United States]."[34] Indeed, the Taliban later became famous for providing a safe haven for Osama bin Laden, who soon became known as the mastermind behind various terrorist acts against American targets.

CHAPTER 5

Paying the Price

In the 1990s and into the new millennium, the consequences of earlier U.S. Middle East policies begin to multiply as Arab and Islamic leaders who once were U.S. allies turned against it. The U.S. responded by using its military power in several conflicts in the Middle East, in some cases with little international support. These incidents fueled a growing animosity toward America and its interests around the world.

Disarming an Ex-Ally—
the Persian Gulf War

In Iraq the former U.S. ally, dictator Saddam Hussein, used his military strength to attack one of his neighbors. Saddam, seeking to revive the Iraqi economy after the Iran-Iraq War, was angered by Kuwait's overproduction of oil, which brought down oil prices. For this reason, Iraq invaded Kuwait on August 2, 1990, and quickly seized control of the country.

The UN Security Council immediately condemned the invasion and called for Iraq to withdraw. Most Arab nations also condemned Iraq. U.S. president George H.W. Bush called the invasion an "outrageous and brutal act of aggression."[35] When Saddam refused to withdraw from Kuwait, the United States put together a coalition within the United Nations that included traditional U.S. European allies as well as Turkey, Saudi Arabia, and many other Arab nations. This group imposed economic sanctions on Iraq, placing strict limits on the country's exports and imports in an attempt to force Saddam to withdraw and disarm. When Saddam still did not leave Kuwait, the coalition, with UN approval, launched a massive

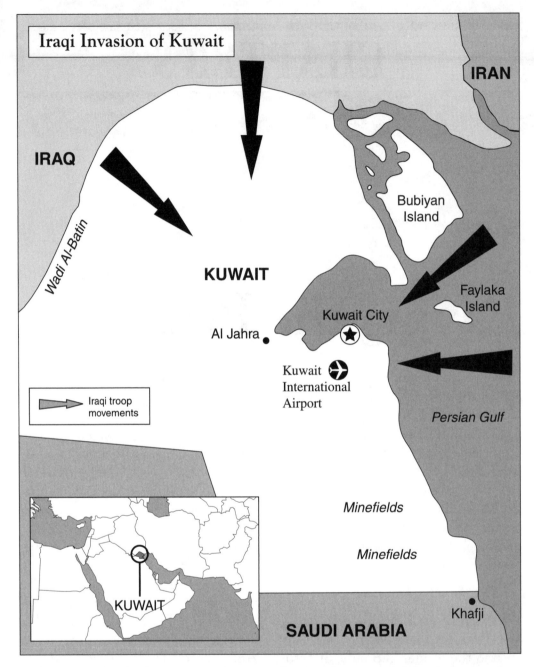

Iraqi Invasion of Kuwait

IRAN

IRAQ

Wadi Al-Batin

Bubiyan Island

KUWAIT

Faylaka Island

Kuwait City

Al Jahra

Kuwait International Airport

Iraqi troop movements

Persian Gulf

Minefields

Minefields

KUWAIT

Khafji

SAUDI ARABIA

military attack called Operation Desert Storm on January 16, 1991.

The attack, which became known as the Persian Gulf War, lasted only a few months. The allied forces quickly liberated Kuwait and destroyed most of Iraq's military arsenal (including nuclear and chemical facilities), much of which had been supplied earlier by the United States and its allies. However, the war also destroyed much of Iraq's urban infrastructure, including irrigation, water, and sewage systems, causing lack of clean water, disease, and food shortages.

After the war, the United Nations voted to keep sanctions in place until all of Iraq's weapons of mass destruction (WMD) programs were destroyed. A weapons inspection team, called the UN Special Commission on Iraq (UNSCOM), was assembled to monitor the disarming, and in the years that followed, UNSCOM uncovered and destroyed much of Iraq's WMD arsenal. Saddam Hussein's aggression was kept in check by these programs, but the devastating effects of the war and the UN sanctions were felt by the Iraqi people throughout the 1990s.

During the years after the war, the United States maintained a military presence in Iraq and conducted numerous air and missile strikes on Iraqi targets. Some argued, however, that unlike the initial strike on Iraq in 1991, which was authorized by the United Nations, the United States conducted these later military actions on its own initiative and therefore they were illegal. For this reason, in the years following the Kuwait invasion, the United States often found itself without the support of allies in Europe or the Arab states on issues relating to Iraq.

Ironically, the Gulf War was in many ways the direct result of America's earlier

Coalition troops flush out Iraqi soldiers in Kuwait during the 1991 Persian Gulf War.

decision to support and arm Saddam Hussein. The weapons the United States gave him to fight Iran in the 1980s were now used against the U.S.-led coalition. Thus, the U.S. practice of arming leaders whose trustworthiness was uncertain was called into question. Indeed, the United States was heavily criticized for having made such shortsighted decisions regarding the Iraqi leader.

Jihad Against America

The American-led attack on Iraq was publicly justified by President Bush as

Osama bin Laden leads a global anti-U.S. terrorism network.

a war to combat aggression by a brutal dictator, and an effort to create a "New World Order . . . where the rule of law, and not the law of the jungle, governs the conduct of nations."[36] As part of this campaign to justify the Persian Gulf War as a humanitarian undertaking, Bush characterized Saddam Hussein as an evil dictator and encouraged the people of Iraq to rebel against his regime. However, when Iraqis revolted against Saddam at the end of the war, President Bush failed to support them, and Saddam Hussein crushed the rebellion, brutally murdering thousands. Bush said the UN authorization for war did not include regime change, and the United States could not assume responsibility for democratizing and rebuilding Iraq. Many see this as proof that America's involvement in the Persian Gulf War was less an effort to bring freedom and democracy to Iraq and more an effort to preserve stability in the Middle East.

In particular, the United States mainly sought to prevent Saddam from trying to take over U.S. oil interests, especially Saudi oil fields. To this end, President Bush was able to secure permission to send tens of thousands of U.S. troops to Saudi Arabia, despite the fact that most Saudis did not want American troops on their soil. Many of these troops remained after the war's end, which led to yet another backlash against the United States.

The presence of large numbers of American troops in Saudi Arabia, an Islamic country, and the Saudi government's acceptance of that presence, out-

Reactions of Arab Countries to the U.S. War on Terror

After the September 11, 2001, attacks, the United States urged Arab countries in the Middle East to crack down on terrorism. This posed a challenge for many Arab governments, because there was widespread support for al Qaeda among many within the Arab and Muslim world. Nevertheless, U.S.-allied states such as Egypt, Saudi Arabia, Jordan, and Pakistan shared intelligence information with the United States and promised to help prevent terrorists from getting funding. For example, as quoted by CNN in June 2003, Egyptian president Hosni Mubarak promised, "We will use the full force of the law to stop funds getting to illegal organizations including terrorist groups."

Under U.S. pressure, even Saudi Arabia, often a financial supporter of terrorism and home to a number of the terrorists who carried out the September 11 attacks, began a significant campaign to arrest terrorists and prevent their access to weapons. Saudi efforts intensified after they experienced terrorism on their own soil. In May and November of 2003, car bombs exploded in several housing complexes around Saudi Arabia, killing many Arabs and Muslims. These attacks, attributed to al Qaeda, diminished the support in Saudi Arabia for Osama bin Laden. As Saudi professor Saad A. Sowayan said in a November 10, 2003, *New York Times* article, "They [al Qaeda] can no longer say they are more or less raising the banner of jihad [holy war] . . . Jihad is not against your own people."

Some of the less moderate Arab states, however, did not support the war on terror, and are believed to be continuing their support of terrorist groups. Syria, for example, is suspected by the United States of helping Islamic militants fight against American troops in Iraq. The nation of Lebanon is also believed to be continuing funding to the terrorist group Hezbollah, whose militants attack Israel.

---

raged many anti-West Islamic militants. To many of these fundamentalists, Westerners are infidels (that is, nonbelievers) and corrupters of Islamic and Arab values. The presence of Western troops in a country like Saudi Arabia, home to two of the most sacred sites in all of Islam (the holy cities of Mecca and Medina), was considered a threat to Islam. As a result, Islamic militants declared jihad, or holy war, against U.S. targets. This jihad called on all Muslims to kill Westerners as part of a moral war to preserve Islam. As historian David W. Lesch puts it, "From this fight to rid Saudi Arabia of its infidel presence grew an all-out war against the United States, Israel, and their presumed cohorts in and outside of the Middle East."[37]

The emerging leader of this holy war was Osama bin Laden, who ironically was one of the mujahideen fighters the CIA had supported in Afghanistan. During the war in Afghanistan, bin Laden had created an international organization to provide housing, training, and aid to the many foreign Islamic fighters resisting the Soviet occupation. Later, this organization of Islamic fighters evolved into the group al Qaeda, which in Arabic means "the Base." Throughout the 1990s bin Laden expanded al Qaeda into an extensive operation of terrorist training camps and other support under the protection of the Taliban regime in Afghanistan.

Bin Laden, a member of one of the wealthiest families in Saudi Arabia, strongly objected to the stationing of American troops in Saudi Arabia during the Gulf War. He also generally resented Western influences and control in the Middle East, which he intended to end by pressuring the West to leave. Bin Laden's goal was to transform the Middle East into a region governed by fundamentalist Islamic governments, like the Taliban in Afghanistan or the Islamic Republic in Iran. Al Qaeda began implementing this grand strategy with a series of terrorist attacks on U.S. targets throughout the 1990s. Indeed, Bin Laden openly declared that Muslims should kill Americans, including civilians, in order to get America to abandon its interests in the Middle East.

The first al Qaeda strike came on December 29, 1992, when a bomb at the Gold Mohur Hotel in Yemen killed two tourists and wounded four more. The bomb, however, was intended for one hundred American servicemen who were in the area. The next year, on February 26, 1993, al Qaeda took the battle to the shores of the United States, bombing the World Trade Center in New York City. This attack killed six people and injured more than one thousand, but did not do as much damage as the terrorists had hoped. Bin Laden next began supplying weapons to fighters in the African nation of Somalia, who on October 3 and 4, 1993, engaged in a fierce battle that left eighteen U.S. servicemen dead in the city of Mogadishu. Terrorism continued in Saudi Arabia with a car bomb on November 13, 1995, at a U.S.-run training facility in Saudi Arabia that killed five Americans and two Indians. All of these attacks were meant to compel the United States to get out of the Middle East and precipitate a tide of Islamic revolution throughout the region.

Al Qaeda's terrorist strikes soon became more deadly, dramatic, and organized. On June 25, 1996, for example, a truck bomb at an apartment compound in Dhahran, Saudi Arabia, where hundreds of U.S. Air Force personnel were stationed, killed 19 U.S. airmen and wounded hundreds more. On August 7, 1998, more truck bombs hit U.S. embassies in Tanzania and Kenya, killing 224, including 12 Americans. On August 12, 2000, a boat containing explosives rammed the USS *Cole* in Yemen, killing 17 sailors and wounding more than 30.

Finally, on September 11, 2001, al Qaeda pulled off its largest and most spectacular strike against America. On that day, four passenger airliners hijacked by al Qaeda terrorists crashed into New York City's World Trade Center, the Pentagon, and a field in rural Pennsylvania, killing a total of 2,752 people, and injuring thousands more.

New York's World Trade Center towers collapse in billows of smoke after terrorists fly airliners into them in 2001. The deadly attacks led to the U.S. war on terrorism.

The War on Terrorism Begins

The tragedy of September 11 was seen as a victory by fundamentalists in the Muslim and Arab world. Although a majority of Muslims felt sympathy for the victims of the attacks, many also saw the attacks as payback for past U.S. policies that had often caused Arab blood to be spilled. As political analyst Yossef Bodansky explains, "For the vast majority of Muslims—irrespective of their position in society or their view of [Islamic fundamentalism]—the desperate heroism of the

The Doctrine of Preemption

On September 20, 2002, President George W. Bush outlined a new national security policy that permits the United States to take preemptive, or preventative, action against terrorists and countries that possess or are developing weapons of mass destruction. The new policy of preemption is a shift from past U.S. policy, which allowed U.S. military action only for defensive purposes.

The report, "The National Security Strategy of the United States," September 17, 2002, can be accessed at www.whitehouse.gov/ncs/nss.html. It explains that with the end of the Cold War between the Soviet Union and the United States, the new threats to U.S. security are from unstable nations (sometimes called rogue states) and terrorists, who may use weapons of mass destruction against the United States and its allies. The report concludes that, "Given the goals of rogue states and terrorists, the United States can no longer solely rely on a reactive posture as we have in the past. The inability to deter a potential attacker, the immediacy of today's threats, and the magnitude of potential harm that could be caused by our adversaries' choice of weapons, do not permit that option. We cannot let our enemies strike first."

The policy of preemption was employed in the U.S. attacks on Afghanistan and Iraq. Critics of these actions, however, have argued that preemption is a dangerous policy. By giving the United States license to attack other countries, critics say, the new policy could lead other countries to adopt similar aggressive policies against the United States or other nations, leading only to greater instability in the world.

President George W. Bush reveals his policy of preemption against terrorism in a 2002 speech.

U.S. Marines secure a position in Afghanistan in 2001. Ousting the terrorist-abetting Afghan government was the first move in the war on terrorism.

perpetrators [of September 11], their embrace of martyrdom, brought a sense of pride."[38] By hitting the World Trade Center, the center of American financial might, and the Pentagon, the center of American military might, the terrorists struck at the very heart of American power. Indeed, after the attacks there was an outpouring of support for Osama bin Laden among Muslims throughout the world, especially among Muslims who felt they had suffered from American policies. In the West Bank, for example, Palestinians who had fought the U.S.-funded Israeli military for many years celebrated, firing guns into the air, honking their car horns, and chanting, "Let the Americans know the meaning of death."[39]

For the United States, the September 11, 2001, terrorist attack was a turning point for its Middle East policies. From this point on, as political science professor Mahmood Monshipouri notes, U.S. policy, in addition to protecting oil resources and supporting Israel, "expanded to include other objectives such as combating terrorism . . . and preventing the spread of weapons of mass destruction (WMD)."[40] Indeed, shortly after the terrorist attack, on September 20, 2001, President George W. Bush declared war on terrorism in an address to Congress and the nation, promising to use every resource and tool, even war, to disrupt and defeat the global terror network. Bush stated, "We will pursue nations that provide aid or safe haven to terrorism. Every nation, in every region, now has a decision to make. Either you are with us, or you are with the terrorists. From this day forward, any nation that continues to harbor or support terrorism will be regarded by the United States as a hostile regime."[41]

This principle was soon employed by the United States to attack and remove offending governments in the Middle East. Shortly after Bush's speech, for example, the United States targeted Afghanistan's Taliban government, who was hosting terrorist mastermind Osama bin Laden and other members of al Qaeda. The U.S. demanded that the Taliban turn over al Qaeda terrorists to the United States and close all terrorist bases in the country. The Taliban regime refused to do so and as a result, on October 7, 2001, the United States, backed by its ally Britain, attacked Afghanistan. Over the next few months the U.S. and British forces ousted the Taliban regime and destroyed al Qaeda bases there. However, bin Laden escaped along with many of his closest aides and Taliban supporters. In addition, the United States has faced severe challenges rebuilding Afghanistan. Many Afghans continue to struggle, while remaining pockets of Taliban and al Qaeda forces carry out attacks around the country, preventing it from stabilizing and developing.

The U.S. War Against Iraq

President Bush next moved the war on terror to Iraq. On January 29, 2002, Bush warned of another facet of terrorism—an "axis of evil," which he said consisted of three countries: Iraq, Iran, and North Korea. He accused these states of seeking to develop weapons of mass destruction and said they posed "a grave and growing danger"[42] because they could provide these weapons to terrorists, attack U.S. allies, or blackmail the United States. President Bush justified military action against such countries under a new policy of preemption, which allowed the United States to take action against countries that pose no present threat but may, at some time in the future, threaten the United States.

Regarding Iraq, Bush argued that Saddam Hussein must be removed from power quickly because he was developing weapons of mass destruction, including nuclear capability. It was also suspected that Iraq had ties to terrorists. One of the Bush administration's main concerns was that Saddam Hussein, if he had advanced weapons, could threaten U.S. oil interests. In a speech in August 2002, for example, Vice President Dick Cheney warned,

Armed with an arsenal of these weapons of terror, and seated atop ten percent of the world's oil reserves, Saddam Hussein could then be expected to seek domination of the entire Middle East, take control of a great portion of the world's energy supplies, directly threaten America's friends throughout the region, and subject the United States or any other nation to nuclear blackmail.[43]

However, the U.S. plan for attacking Iraq was widely denounced, both in America and around the world. Bush's critics said there was a lack of information about Iraq's weapons programs; indeed, whether Saddam Hussein possessed weapons of mass destruction was unclear. Others questioned the policy of preemption, arguing that it reversed previous U.S. efforts to limit military action. They also worried that aggression on America's part would give other countries the license to be irresponsibly aggressive toward their enemies.

Iraqi dictator Saddam Hussein's regime fell to U.S.-led forces in 2003.

U.S. soldiers search for enemy hideouts in Iraq. The U.S.-led invasion of Iraq was opposed by the United Nations and by many in America and throughout the world.

Still others critical of war in Iraq argued that there was no plan to stabilize Iraq after Saddam was removed from power, and that the cost of war and rebuilding would be astronomical. Finally, the link between Iraq and terrorism was not decisively proved, and it was argued that fighting an unnecessary war against Iraq could actually weaken the war on terrorism.

As the United States pushed to lead a UN coalition in a war against Iraq, other members of the UN Security Council, including some who had been part of the 1991 coalition, spoke out against it. Nations such as Russia, Ger-

many, and France recommended more time for weapons inspection and urged the council not to approve war unless proof was found that Iraq had weapons of mass destruction. Moderate Arab states such as Saudi Arabia and Jordan also opposed war because it would likely cause anti-American uprisings in their countries.

Yet, on March 19, 2002, without UN support and in spite of massive peace demonstrations in the United States and around the world, the United States and a few allies, including Britain and Australia, began to wage war against Iraq. They achieved a quick victory with an overwhelming display of American firepower and force—enough to serve as a warning to other nations not to act against U.S. interests.

The Bush administration's main justification for the war was to rid Iraq of WMDs. Yet, months after the war, American search teams had still not found any WMDs in Iraq. In addition, the Bush administration repeatedly rejected calls for UN involvement in rebuilding Iraq and instead awarded initial reconstruction contracts to American firms with close connections to the administration. Critics therefore suggested that the real reasons for the war were to control Iraqi oil, to profit from doing business in Iraq after the war, and to install a government in Iraq that would be open to U.S. influence.

Stung by this criticism, President Bush began emphasizing the hope that America offers to Middle Eastern countries for democracy and freedom. In November 2003, he announced a new American policy of promoting democratic reforms in the Middle East. Bush said, "Sixty years of Western nations excusing and accommodating the lack of freedom in the Middle East did nothing to make us safe, because in the long run stability cannot be purchased at the expense of liberty. As long as the Middle East remains a place where freedom

This crater was made by a car bomb blown up outside an Iraqi police station in 2003. Continuing anti-U.S. terrorism in Iraq plagues rebuilding efforts.

does not flourish, it will remain a place of stagnation, resentment and violence ready for export."[44] However, the inadequacy of U.S. postwar nation-building plans and the U.S. reluctance to allow Iraqis to hold an open election convinced many that nation building and democracy were not America's first priorities.

Growing Anti-U.S. Terrorism in Iraq

As months passed, reconstruction in Iraq proceeded slowly, hampered by the lack of security and sabotage attacks on newly repaired electrical facilities and oil pipelines. In the fall of 2003 guerrilla fighters escalated attacks against U.S. troops and Iraqis trying to stabilize the country. The attackers at first shot at U.S. soldiers and planted land mines to blow up their vehicles. Tactics quickly grew to include shocking suicide bombings of UN and humanitarian aid headquarters and more sophisticated missile strikes on U.S. helicopters.

Bush administration officials initially claimed that the attackers were former members of Saddam Hussein's government who were still loyal and wanted to return him to power, assisted by criminals who were being paid to carry out attacks. Later, however, officials determined that the anti-American resistance also included foreign fighters who were sneaking into Iraq from other places. Some reports said that, as happened during the Soviet occupation of Afghanistan, a wave of Muslim militants was headed to Iraq in response to the call of terrorists, such as Osama bin Laden, for Muslims to join the jihad, or holy war, against the American-led occupation. If true, Iraq could become a big problem for America, with increasing numbers of U.S. troop casualties.

Indeed, although initially billed by the Bush administration as part of the war on terrorism, the Iraq War may in the end increase terrorist activity against America and its interests. As political analysts Daniel Benjamin and Steven Simon caution, "As long as [U.S.] troops must attend to protecting themselves and tracking insurgents instead of setting [Iraq] aright, the U.S.'s claims of being a beneficent liberator will ring hollow in the ears of many Muslims. And they in turn may find the al-Qaeda view of the universe increasingly attractive."[45]

Growing Distrust in American Involvement

A scandal that unfolded in the spring of 2004 concerning the treatment of Iraqi prisoners provoked further challenges to Bush administration claims that America was truly the liberator of the Iraqi people. As increasing numbers of suspected insurgents were rounded up, the U.S. military detained them for questioning in various facilities around Iraq. Some detention centers were makeshift camps in the desert; others were fortified prisons formerly used as torture centers during Saddam's regime.

Although coalition forces were bound by internationally accepted conventions to treat prisoners humanely, in May 2004 it came to light that terrible abuses had been committed in at least one American-controlled Iraqi detention facility. Photographs surfaced showing U.S. soldiers cheerfully posing beside Iraqi prisoners who had been stripped naked and forced into uncomfortable positions or stacked in piles. Other photographs showed naked Iraqis being attacked by police dogs and otherwise terrorized or humiliated. One hooded prisoner, for example, was photographed balancing on a small box with a noose around his neck and electric wires attached to his hands; the prisoner was reportedly threatened with electrocution if he lowered his arms or fell off the box. Even more disturbing reports described the sexual abuse of inmates by soldiers, including rape.

It was unclear if a few corrupt soldiers had acted on their own initiative or if the atrocities had been sanctioned by high-ranking military officials. In any case, the abuse of prisoners was decried around the world. Shocked and outraged responses called into question the morality of the American mission in Iraq, whose stated goal had been to end the era of torture Iraqis had suffered under Saddam.

President Bush condemned the prisoner abuse as being inconsistent with American values and the honorable record of the armed forces in Iraq. Congress launched an inquiry into the scandal, vowing to bring those responsible to justice. These efforts, however, did not quell the anger of the Iraqi people. Indeed, the insurgency intensified after the abuse scandal came to light, as militants vowed revenge on military personnel and American civilians alike.

Across the Middle East, anti-American sentiment was increasingly vehement. Those who had never supported the American-led war in Iraq cited the prison abuses as proof that Americans had come to Iraq not as liberators, but as a brutal occupying force. Others predicted that the images of American soldiers mistreating the prisoners would serve as recruitment posters for terrorists. Indeed, among radical factions in the Middle East, cries for revenge rang out. However, more moderate sectors of Middle Eastern society condemned the abuses but praised the United States for launching an investigation to identify and prosecute those responsible. It is exactly such openness and regard for the truth, they argued, that make democracy worth pursuing.

At the very least, the prisoner abuse scandal further tarnished America's reputation in the Middle East. It also made the already daunting task of nation building that much more difficult. By May 2004, the situation in Iraq was dangerously unsettled, and Iraqis seemed a long way from peace and stability.

The United States as Mediator of the Arab-Israeli Dispute

The U.S. actions in Iraq and Afghanistan, and the larger war on terror, are intimately linked to the problem of Israeli-Arab relations. America's support for Israel and its inability to resolve the Palestinian problem is the original source of much of the anti-American sentiment in the Arab-Muslim world.

Indeed, the U.S. failure to resolve the Israeli-Palestinian conflict in the fifty-plus years since Israel's birth is seen by many as a major cause of rising anti-American terrorism and a big part of the reason the United States faces opposition in countries like Iraq and Afghanistan.

Over the years, numerous attempts by the United States and the parties themselves to mediate a solution to the Arab-Israeli conflict have repeatedly failed, leaving Palestinians increasingly desperate and provoking major and violent Palestinian uprisings, called intifadas, in the Israeli-occupied territories. After the U.S. victory in the 2003 war against Iraq, the United States once again claimed the role of mediator and promised to seek a permanent solution to the Arab-Israeli conflict. From the outset of these negotiations, however, the United States condemned the Palestinian leadership as too extreme to work with, and forced Palestinians to elect new leaders. Notably, at the same time as the United States was insisting on a moderate representative for the Palestinians, it fully supported Israeli prime minister Ariel Sharon, whom many view as an extremist. It is this kind of imbalanced treatment in the Israeli-Palestinian saga that helps perpetuate the conflict and generate anti-U.S. sentiment.

Democracy in the Middle East

Throughout the history of U.S. involvement in the Middle East, the United States has been criticized for aligning itself with nations such as Saudi Arabia, Jordan, Egypt, and Pakistan, which do not have democratic systems of government. The United States has been willing to deal with stable dictators rather than potentially unstable, democratically elected politicians, despite the restrictions or oppression such dictatorships imposed on their own people.

On November 6, 2003, however, U.S. president George W. Bush made history by calling for democratic freedoms in the Middle East. Bush also said the United States accepted some of the blame for the lack of freedom in the region and urged Middle Eastern governments to promote and implement democratic reforms:

In many Middle Eastern countries poverty is deep and it is spreading, women lack rights and are denied schooling, whole societies remain stagnant while the world moves ahead. These are not the failures of a culture or a religion. These are the failures of political and economic doctrines. . . . Instead of dwelling on past wrongs and blaming others, governments in the Middle East need to confront real problems and serve the true interests of their nations.

Many critics suspected however, that Bush seized on the democracy theme as a new justification for America's war in Iraq. Bush's first justification for the war, that Iraq was developing weapons of mass destruction, was questioned when U.S. teams were unable to find any such weapons

Iranian demonstrators burn a U.S. flag in Tehran in 2003. Animosity toward the United States continues to grow in the Middle East.

In this way, many in the Middle East believe that the United States has denied peace and justice to Arabs and Muslims in the region. This sentiment has tarnished America's reputation in the Middle East. As political scientist Amin Saikal explains,

The US embrace of Israel as a strategic partner within a decade of its creation, matched by a commitment to guarantee its security irrespective of its effect on the Palestinians in particular and the Arab-Muslim world in general, has been a misjudgement of gigantic proportions. It may have been beneficial to [United States] domestic and Cold War politics, but only at the cost of tension and turbulence in America's relations with the Muslim world.[46]

The United States thus has come full circle, to the point where its own policies, designed to protect American interests, have in the end helped make it a target for terror.

The Cost to America

At the beginning of the twenty-first century, U.S. Middle East policies have had an increasingly heavy cost to Americans. Over the years, U.S. policies have helped inspire a dangerous and growing anger that in recent times has exploded in the form of terrorism. Violence against America, in turn, led the United States into the war on terror which many people in the region believe is a war on Islam.

No matter its intentions, the U.S. involvement in the Middle East has had far-reaching and often unintended repercussions. In its efforts to maintain regional security, the United States often overlooked the desires of the region's population. This in turn has fueled anti-American sentiment throughout the Middle East, and has encouraged radical terrorist groups such as al Qaeda to target American interests.

NOTES

Chapter 1: The Roots of American Interests in the Middle East

1. Quoted in Sheldon L. Richman, "'Ancient History': U.S. Conduct in the Middle East Since World War II and the Folly of Intervention," Cato Institute, August 16, 1999. www.cato.org/pubs/pas/pa-159es.html.

2. The Avalon Project at Yale Law School, "The Truman Doctrine: President Harry S. Truman's Address Before a Joint Session of Congress, March 12, 1947," www.yale.edu/lawweb/avalon/tru doc.htm.

3. Quoted in George Lenczowski, *American Presidents and the Middle East*. Durham, SC: Duke University Press, 1990, p. 21.

4. Quoted in Samih K. Farsoun and Christina E. Zacharia, *Palestine and the Palestinians*. Boulder, CO: Westview, 1997, p. 72.

5. Quoted in George W. Ball and Douglas B. Ball, *The Passionate Attachment*. New York: W.W. Norton, 1992, p. 20.

6. Quoted in Lenczowski, *American Presidents and the Middle East*, p. 30.

7. Richman, "'Ancient History.'"

8. Quoted in Richman, "'Ancient History.'"

Chapter 2: America as the Dominant Middle East Power

9. Quoted in Lenczowski, *American Presidents and the Middle East*, p. 37.

10. Tore T. Peterson, *The Middle East Between the Great Powers*. New York: St. Martin's, 2000, p. 67.

11. Lenczowski, *American Presidents and the Middle East*, 1990, p. 46.

12. Avi Shlaim, *War and Peace in the Middle East*. New York: Whittle Books, 1994, p. 31.

13. Internet Modern History Sourcebook, "President Eisenhower: The Eisenhower Doctrine on the Middle East, a Message to Congress, January 5, 1957," www.fordham.edu/halsall/mod/1957eisenhower doctrine.html.

14. Quoted in Lenczowski, *American Presidents and the Middle East*, p. 63.

15. Lenczowski, *American Presidents and the Middle East*, p. 63.

Chapter 3: Sowing the Seeds of Conflict—the Johnson and Nixon Years

16. Ian J. Bickerton and Carla L. Klausner, *A Concise History of the Arab-Israeli Conflict*. Upper Saddle River, NJ: Prentice-Hall, 2002, p. 151.
17. Lenczowski, *American Presidents and the Middle East*, p. 112.
18. Quoted in Ball and Ball, *The Passionate Attachment*, p. 60.
19. Richman, "'Ancient History.'"
20. Quoted in Lenczowski, *American Presidents and the Middle East*, p. 127.
21. Lenczowski, *American Presidents and the Middle East*, p. 130.
22. Richman, "'Ancient History.'"
23. Quoted in Lenczowski, *American Presidents and the Middle East*, p. 118.

Chapter 4: Fallout from U.S. Policies—the Beginning of Anti-U.S. Terrorism

24. Quoted in Bernard Reich, "The United States and Israel: The Nature of a Special Relationship," ed. David W. Lesch, *The Middle East and the United States*. Boulder, CO: Westview, 2003, p. 233.
25. Quoted in Ball and Ball, *The Passionate Attachment*, p. 108.
26. Shlaim, *War and Peace in the Middle East*, p. 55.
27. Quoted in Mark Tessler, *A History of the Israeli-Palestinian Conflict*, Bloomington: Indiana University Press, 1994, p. 638.
28. Shlaim, *War and Peace in the Middle East*, p. 58.
29. Shlaim, *War and Peace in the Middle East*, p. 59.
30. David W. Lesch, *1979: The Year That Shaped the Modern Middle East.* Boulder, CO: Westview, 2001, p. 63.
31. Quoted in Dilip Hiro, *The Longest War: The Iran-Iraq Military Conflict.* New York: Routledge Chapman & Hall, 1991, p. 35.
32. Con Coughlin, *Saddam: King of Terror.* New York: HarperCollins, 2002, p. 238.
33. Quoted in Lenczowski, *American Presidents and the Middle East*, p. 206.
34. Lesch, *1979*, p. 104.

Chapter 5: Paying the Price

35. Quoted in Coughlin, *Saddam*, p. 256.
36. Quoted in Shlaim, *War and Peace in the Middle East*, p. 129.
37. Lesch, *1979*, p. 104.
38. Yossef Bodansky, *The High Cost of Peace.* Roseville, CA: Prima, 2002, p. 503.
39. Quoted in Bodansky, *The High Cost of Peace*, p. 504.
40. Mahmood Monshipouri, "The Paradoxes of U.S. Policy in the Middle East," *Middle East Policy*, September 2002.
41. George W. Bush, address to Joint Session of Congress, Washington, DC, September 20, 2001. www.usinfo.state.gov.
42. George W. Bush, State of the Union address, Washington, DC, January 29, 2002. www.usinfo.state.gov.

43. Dick Cheney, speech to Veterans of Foreign Wars 103rd National Convention, August 26, 2002. www.guardian.co.uk/Iraq/Story/0,2 763,781216,00.html.

44. Quoted in *New York Times*, "In Bush's Words: 'Iraqi Democracy Will Succeed,'" November 6, 2003.

45. Daniel Benjamin and Steven Simon, "The Real Worry: In Iraq We Have Created a New 'Field of Jihad,'" *Time*, September 1, 2003.

46. Amin Saikal, *Islam and the West: Conflict or Cooperation?* New York: Palgrave Macmillan, 2003, p. 89.

CHRONOLOGY

1517
The Ottoman Empire conquers Palestine.

1880s
The first Jewish settlers arrive in Palestine.

1901
Oil is first discovered in Persia.

1916
Britain and France sign the Sykes-Picot Agreement, giving Britain control over Palestine after the World War I.

1917
Britain issues the Balfour Declaration; at the end of World War I, Britain invades Palestine and establishes a military occupation.

1919
Britain and America set up the King-Crane Commission to investigate the situation in Palestine.

1920
The Allied powers meet at a conference in San Remo, Italy, and decide to give Britain a mandate to rule Palestine; Arab protests follow.

1930s
The Arabs wage an armed struggle against both the British and the Jewish settlers in Palestine.

1938
Oil is discovered in Saudi Arabia, Bahrain, and Kuwait by American oil companies.

1939
World War II begins; Britain issues the White Paper, which restricts Jewish immigration.

1941–1945
The German Nazis conduct the Holocaust, seeking to destroy all Jews in Europe; in Palestine, Jewish guerrilla groups (Irgun, the Stern Gang) conduct attacks on the British throughout World War II.

1945
The Soviet Union tries to take control of Iran after the end of World War II but is convinced to leave by American threats.

1946
Anglo-American Committee of Inquiry recommends that one hundred thousand Jews be admitted into Palestine

and that the area become a binational state for both Jews and Arabs.

1947

The Soviet Union seeks control in Turkey and Greece; the Truman Doctrine provides for U.S. military and economic aid in the Middle East to prevent the spread of communism; the United Nations approves the partition of Palestine into separate Jewish and Palestinian states.

1948

Israel declares its independence.

1950

Muhammad Mossadeq nationalizes Iran's oil industry; the United States intervenes to restore the shah of Iran to power.

1953

Egyptian president Gamal Abdel Nasser demands that Britain withdraw all its troops from its military base on the Suez Canal; the United States mediates the dispute.

1955

Turkey, Iraq, Pakistan, Iran, and Britain sign a northern tier defense agreement called the Baghdad Pact; Egypt refuses to sign and turns to the Soviet Union for arms.

1956

The United States refuses to fund a project at the Aswan Dam in Egypt; Nasser nationalizes the Suez Canal; Israel, with the help of France and Britain, attacks Egypt, starting the Suez-Sinai War.

1957

U.S. president Eisenhower announces the Eisenhower Doctrine, which authorizes him to use U.S. armed forces to prevent imminent or actual aggression from Communist forces anywhere in the Middle East; Jordan's pro-Western government, with U.S. aid, repels a challenge from socialist-nationalists aided by the Communist Party; Turkish and U.S. intervention stops Baath and Communist radicals from taking over Syria's government.

1958

A coalition of pro-Nasser Muslim and radical forces rebel against Lebanese president Camille Chamoun, but is repelled when U.S. troops are sent to Lebanon; the monarchy in Iraq is overthrown in a military coup led by General Karim Kassem, a Nasser supporter.

1962

A group of pro-Nasser army officers under the leadership of Colonel Abdullah al-Sallal topples the pro-British Yemen monarchy.

1963

Cyprus president Archbishop Makarios takes action against the Turkish minority; the United States prevents Turkey from intervening.

1967

The Six-Day War begins and ends with Israel's occupation of the West Bank, Gaza, the Sinai, and the Golan Heights.

1968

The Baath Party comes to power in Iraq; Britain announces it will withdraw its military forces from the Persian Gulf; the United States develops its Twin Pillars policy, asking Iran and Saudi Arabia to be its defenders in the Middle East.

1970
Civil war begins in Jordan over eviction of the Palestine Liberation Organization (PLO); the United States authorizes Israel to stop Syria from intervening.

1972
U.S. relations with Turkey deteriorate after the U.S. Congress cuts off military aid to Turkey.

1973
Egyptian and Syrian forces attack Israel, starting the Yom Kippur War; Arab states begin the Arab Oil Embargo.

1978
Following negotiations mediated by U.S. president Jimmy Carter, Israel and Egypt sign a peace agreement called the Camp David Accords which leads to a separate peace treaty between Egypt and Israel.

1979
The Islamic Revolution begins in Iran; Iranian militants take sixty-six Americans hostage; the Soviet Union invades Afghanistan; the United States covertly provides military assistance and arms to Islamic mujahideen to help them fight the Soviets.

1980
The Iran-Iraq War begins when Iraq attacks Iran; the United States provides arms to Iraqi leader Saddam Hussein.

1982
Israel invades Lebanon to destroy PLO headquarters; the United States sends troops to Lebanon as peacekeepers, leading to terrorist attacks on American troops.

1987
The first Palestinian intifada begins.

1988
A UN cease-fire goes into effect to end the Iran-Iraq War.

1990–1991
Iraq invades Kuwait; the United States leads a UN coalition in the first Persian Gulf War to liberate Kuwait and disarm Iraq.

1991
U.S. president George H.W. Bush opens a peace conference in Madrid, Spain, which is attended by Israel and the Arab states.

1993
Israel and the Palestinians sign the Oslo Agreements, giving Palestinians self-rule in portions of the occupied territories.

1994
Jordan and Israel sign a formal peace treaty on October 26.

2000
Palestinian-Israeli peace talks collapse at Camp David, Maryland, summit meeting; the second Palestinian intifada begins.

2001
Al Qaeda terrorists attack American targets around the world, including the World Trade Center in New York City; the United States and Britain launch a war in Afghanistan to eliminate terrorists and overthrow the Taliban regime.

2002
U.S. president George W. Bush announces in State of the Union speech

that Iraq is one of three countries forming an "axis of evil," threatening the world by supporting terrorists and developing weapons of mass destruction.

2003

The United States, with a few allies, begins a war against Iraq, quickly removing the Saddam Hussein regime; reconstruction efforts are slowed by increasing terrorist strikes against American, humanitarian, and Iraqi targets; U.S. president George W. Bush presents the road map peace plan to Israel and the Palestinians, leading to a cease-fire; violence resumes, derailing peace talks; Bush calls for democratic reforms in the Middle East.

FOR FURTHER READING

Books

David J. Abodaher, *Youth in the Middle East: Voices of Despair*. New York: Franklin Watts, 1990. Conversations with young people in the Middle East describe the political situation there and how it has affected them.

Elizabeth Ferber, *Yasir Arafat: A Life of War and Peace*. Brookfield, CT: Millbrook,1995. A biography of Yasir Arafat, leader of the PLO and the Palestinian people.

John Charles Griffiths, *The Conflict in Afghanistan*. Vero Beach, FL: Rourke Enterprises, 1989. A discussion of the conflict in Afghanistan following the invasion by the Soviets.

Laurel Holliday, *Why Do They Hate Me?: Young Lives Caught in War and Conflict*. New York: Pocket Books, 1999. A collection of nonfiction essays about children in violent conflicts such as the Holocaust and the Israeli-Palestinian war.

Elaine Landau, *Osama bin Laden: A War Against the West*. Brookfield, CT: Twenty-first Century Books, 2002. A biography of terrorist Osama bin Laden, discussing his beliefs and his role in international terrorism.

Ann Morris, *When Will the Fighting Stop?: A Child's View of Jerusalem*. New York: Atheneum, 1990. A story about a young Jewish boy living in Jerusalem who wonders why all the different people in the city cannot all be friends.

Jill C. Wheeler, *September 11, 2001: The Day That Changed America*. Edina, MN: Abdo, 2002. Describes the events and immediate aftermath of the September 11, 2001, terrorist attacks on the United States.

Internet Sources

Mideast Web, "Middle East History and Resources." www.mideastweb.org/history.htm. This site is operated by a nonprofit group that attempts to provide balanced information on the Middle East conflict, with articles and information from both Palestinian and Israeli sources.

University at Albany, "History in the News: The Middle East." www.albany.edu/history/middle-east. A New York State University site providing links to resources for a study of the Middle East.

U.S. Department of State International Information Programs, "The Middle East: A Vision for the Future." http://usinfo.state.gov/regional/nea/ summit. This U.S.government site provides information about the 2003 Middle East peace process, as well as related information such as a chronology and glossary.

World History Compass, "The Middle East." www.worldhistorycompass. com/meast.htm. Provides links to sites for various countries in the Middle East.

Web Sites

Foundation for Middle East Peace (www.fmep.org). A site run by a nonprofit organization dedicated to informing Americans about the Israeli-Palestinian conflict and assisting in a peaceful solution that brings security for both sides.

Middle East Policy Council (www. mepc.org). A nonprofit organization that provides a forum for viewpoints on recent developments that affect U.S. Middle East policy.

United Nations (www.un.org). The official Web site of the United Nations has links to key documents, maps, daily news and other interesting information.

U.S. Department of State Bureau of Near Eastern Affairs (www.state. gov/p/nea).This is a government Web site on U.S. foreign policy and U.S. diplomatic relations with the countries and geographic entities of Algeria, Bahrain, Egypt, Iran, Iraq, Israel, Jordan, Kuwait, Lebanon, Libya, Morocco, Oman, Qatar, Saudi Arabia, Syria, Tunisia, United Arab Emirates, and Yemen.

WORKS CONSULTED

Books

George W. Ball and Douglas B. Ball, *The Passionate Attachment*. New York: W.W. Norton, 1992. This is a critique of America's decades-long relationship with Israel, from 1947 to the early 1990s.

Ian J. Bickerton and Carla L. Klausner, *A Concise History of the Arab-Israeli Conflict*. Upper Saddle River, NJ: Prentice-Hall, 2002. A short but substantive history of the Arab-Israeli conflict from the time of Ottoman rule to the election of Ariel Sharon as prime minister of Israel.

Yossef Bodansky, *The High Cost of Peace*. Roseville, CA: Prima, 2002. A critique of U.S. involvement in the Arab-Israeli peace process and its connection to anti-American terrorist attacks.

John K. Cooley, *Payback: America's Long War in the Middle East*. New York: Brassey's, 1991. A review of the effects of various U.S. Middle East policies, including American reliance on the shah of Iran, American military support for Iraq, and U.S. assistance to Israel during its invasion of Lebanon.

Con Coughlin, *Saddam: King of Terror*. New York: HarperCollins, 2002. A biography of Saddam Hussein, who ruled Iraq for decades until the United States overthrew his regime in 2003.

Samih K. Farsoun and Christina E. Zacharia, *Palestine and the Palestinians*. Boulder, CO: Westview, 1997. This book provides an analysis of the political development of the Palestine people from early times to their modern demands for statehood.

Dilip Hiro, *The Longest War: The Iran-Iraq Military Conflict*. New York: Routledge Chapman & Hall, 1991. A detailed discussion of the Iran-Iraq War, its causes, and ramifications.

George Lenczowski, *American Presidents and the Middle East*. Durham, SC: Duke University Press, 1990. A comprehensive study of the role U.S. presidents have played in formulating and managing U.S. Middle East policies.

David W. Lesch, ed., *The Middle East and the United States*. Boulder, CO: Westview, 2003. A collection of articles written by scholars and diplomats from the Middle East, Europe, and North America assessing U.S. policy in the Middle East.

———, *1979: The Year That Shaped the Modern Middle East*. Boulder, CO: Westview, 2001. A well-researched book about several pivotal events in 1979, including the Iranian revolution, the Soviet Union's invasion of Afghanistan, and the Egyptian-Israeli peace treaty.

Ritchie Ovendale, *Britain, the United States, and the Transfer of Power in the Middle East, 1945–1962*. New York: Leicester University Press, 1996. An authoritative study of the British role in the Middle East and how British power gave way to American dominance.

Tore T. Peterson, *The Middle East Between the Great Powers*. New York: St. Martin's, 2000. A scholarly review of the decline of British power in the Middle East between 1952 and 1957.

Amin Saikal, *Islam and the West: Conflict or Cooperation?* New York: Palgrave Macmillan, 2003. A discussion of the relationship between Islam and the West.

Avi Shlaim, *War and Peace in the Middle East*. New York: Whittle Books, 1994. An examination of the policies of the Ottoman Empire, European countries, and the United States toward the Middle East.

Howard Teicher and Gayle Radley Teicher, *Twin Pillars to Desert Storm*. New York: William Morrow, 1993. A discussion of U.S. Middle East policy from the Nixon presidency through the first Bush presidency.

Mark Tessler, *A History of the Israeli-Palestinian Conflict*. Bloomington: Indiana University Press, 1994. A comprehensive history of the Arab-Palestinian conflict from the origins of Zionism through the 1987 intifada.

Robin Wright, *The Last Great Revolution: Turmoil and Transformation in Iran*. New York: Vintage Books, 2001. The author, an American journalist, examines the multitude of changes in Iran during the first two decades after the revolution.

Periodicals

Associated Press, "Israeli Raid in Syria Alarms Arab World," *New York Times*, October 6, 2003.

William O. Beeman, "Why Middle Eastern Terrorists Hate the United States," *Synthesis/Regeneration*, Winter 2002.

Daniel Benjamin and Steven Simon, "The Real Worry: In Iraq We Have Created a New 'Field of Jihad,'" *Time*, September 1, 2003.

Economist, "After the War Is Over—Israel and Palestine," April 13, 2002.

Joshua Hammer, "Running Off the Roadmap: Abbas Resigns in Frustration, Leaving Bush's Dreams of Reform in Tatters," *Newsweek*, September 15, 2003.

Rashid Khalidi, "American Anointed: How the United States Sowed the Whirlwind," *American Prospect*, November 19, 2001.

Neil MacFarouhar, "Deadly Bombing of Saudi Homes Sours Al Qaeda Sympathizers," *New York Times*, November 10, 2003.

Mahmood Monshipouri, "The Paradoxes of U.S. Policy in the Middle East," *Middle East Policy*, September 2002.

New York Times, "In Bush's Words: 'Iraqi Democracy Will Succeed,'" November 6, 2003.

Steven R. Weisman, "Betting on Democracy in the Muslim World," *New York Times*, November 9, 2003.

Stephen Zunes, "Foreign Policy by Catharsis: The Failure of U.S. Policy Toward Iraq," *Arab Studies Quarterly*, Fall 2001.

Internet Sources

The Avalon Project at Yale Law School, "The Truman Doctrine: President Harry S. Truman's Address Before a Joint Session of Congress, March 12, 1947," www.yale.edu/lawweb/avalon/trudoc.htm.

Bureau of Public Affairs, U.S. Department of State, "A Performance-Based Roadmap to a Permanent Two-State Solution to the Israeli-Palestinian Conflict," April 30, 2003. www.state.gov/r/pa/prs/ps/2003/20062.htm.

George W. Bush, address to Joint Session of Congress, Washington, DC, September 20, 2001. www.usinfo.state.gov.

———, State of the Union address, Washington, DC, January 29, 2002. www.usinfo.state.gov.

Dick Cheney, speech to Veterans of Foreign Wars 103rd National Convention, August 26, 2002. www.guardian.co.uk/Iraq/Story/0,2763,781216,00.html.

Christian Action for Israel, "The United Nations and Israel: General Assembly Resolution 194," http://christianactionforisrael.org/un/194.html.

CNN, "Arab States Back Road Map," June 3, 2003. http://edition.cnn.com/2003/WORLD/meast/06/03/bush.arabs.

Factmonster, "Pan-Arabism," www.factmonster.com/ce6/history/A0837455.htmlPan-Arabism%20and%20Arab.

Arjan El Fassed, "Were the Palestinians Wrong to Reject the UN Partition Plan?" Laurie King-Irani, ed., Islamic Association for Palestine, www.iap.org/partition.htm.

Federation of American Scientists, "Cold War History," www.fas.org/man/dod-101/ops/docs/coldwar_hist.htm.

Haaretz Daily, "Israel's Road Map Reservations," August 22, 2003. www.haaretzdaily.com/hasen/pages/ShArt.jhtml?itemNo=297230&contrassID=2&subContrassID=1&sbSubContrassID=0&listSrc=Y.

Conn Hallinan, "Road Map: Sharon & the Record," Foreign Policy in Focus, June 20, 2003. www.fpif.org.

Diego Ibarguen and Jonathan S. Landy, "Arab Leaders Pledge to Crack Down on Terror," Knight Ridder Newspapers, June 3, 2003. www.realcities.com/mld/krwashington/news/columnists/jonathan_s_landay/6005963.htm.

Internet Modern History Sourcebook, "President Eisenhower: The Eisenhower Doctrine on the Middle East, a Message to Congress, January 5, 1957," www.fordham.edu/halsall/mod/1957eisenhowerdoctrine.html.

The Middle East Research Project, "The United Nations Partition of Palestine," www.merip.org/palestine-israel_primer/un-partition-plan-pal-isr.html.

"The National Security Strategy of the United States," September 17, 2002. www.whitehouse.gov/nsc/nss.html.

Sheldon L. Richman, "'Ancient History': U.S. Conduct in the Middle East Since World War II and the Folly of Intervention," Cato Institute, August 16, 1999. www.cato.org/pubs/pas/pa-159es.html.

Brian Trumbore, "The Arab Oil Embargo of 1973–74," July 2000. www.buyandhold.com/bh/en/education/history/2002/arab.html.

Wikipedia, "Moammar Al Qadhafi," http://en2.wikipedia.org/wiki/Moammar_Al_Qadhafi.

INDEX

Pan-Arabism and, 43–44
U.S. Middle East policy
and, 19, 21, 22
see also arms race; Cold
War; Soviet Union
Coughlin, Con, 70

Dardanelles, 19
Daud, Sardar Mohammad,
70
dictators, 88
see also specific leaders
Dulles, John Foster, 32, 36

Egypt
Camp David Accords
and, 57–59
Palestine and, 27
Pan-Arabism and, 32–33,
42
Six-Day War and, 45–46
Suez crisis and, 37–40
U.S. policy toward, in
1950s, 35–39
Yom Kippur War and,
51–54
Eisenhower, Dwight D., 29,
30, 37–40
Eisenhower Doctrine,
40–42

Faisal (king of Iraq), 17
Farouk (king of Egypt), 32
France, 15–16
fundamentalist Islamic
movement, 64–65, 66,
76–78
see also Afghanistan; Iran

Gaza, 27, 46, 47
Gemayel, Bashir, 60
Golan Heights, 46, 47, 60
Great Britain
Arab revolts against, 29

colonialism of, in Middle
East, 15–17
Egypt and, 32
Iraq formation and, 17
Iraq War and, 84
Jewish immigration to
Palestine and, 22–23
military withdrawal of,
from Persian Gulf area,
54
Palestine mandate and,
22–25
Suez Canal crisis and,
33–36
Greece, 19, 20, 22
Gulf War (1991), 13,
73–76

Haig, Alexander, 60
hatred. *See* anti-Americanism; terrorism; and *specific
wars*
Hezbollah, 77
Hussein (king of Jordan),
40–41
Hussein, Saddam, 69, 73,
76, 82, 83
see also Iraq

Ibn Sa'ud, 18
intifada, 88
see also Islamic Jihad;
Palestinians; terrorism
Iran
CENTO and, 36
Cold War and, 18–19
communism and, 18–19
hostage crisis in, 66–68
invasion of Oman by,
55–56
Iraq War and, 68–70
Islamic revolution in,
12–13, 32, 36, 63,
64–66

military support for,
54–56
oil crisis of 1950s in,
29–32
revolutionary guards of,
63
Soviet Union and, 18–19
terrorism and, 64–68
Twin Pillars foreign pol-
icy and, 54–56
U.S. relations before
1979, 32
weapons for, 55–56
Iran-Iraq War, 68–70
Iraq
creation of, 17
economic sanctions and,
73–76
Great Britain and, 25
Kuwait invasion by, 73
military development of,
68–70
Pan-Arabism and, 42
Iraq War, 83–84, 86,
86–87
Irgun Zva'i Le'umi, 24
Islam, 77
see also fundamentalist Islamic movement; Is-
lamic revolution
Islamic Jihad, 63, 77–78
Islamic Republic. *See* Iran
Islamic revolution, 63,
65–67, 69
Israel
Camp David Accords
and, 57–59
Cold War and, 28
creation of, 25–27
invasion of Lebanon by,
59–64
Palestinian struggle and,
12–13, 60–61
as proxy for U.S., 50–51

Palestine Liberation Organization (PLO), 50–51, 56
Palestinians, 12–13, 26, 27, 47, 60
Pan-Arabism, 32–33
Partition of 1947. *See* Israel; Palestine
peacekeeping forces, 61–62
see also United Nations; *specific wars*
Pentagon, 78
Persian Gulf War, 13, 73–76
Peterson, Tore T., 37
Petroleum Reserves Company, 18
polarization, of Middle East, 44
see also anti-Americanism
preemption policy, 80, 83
see also terrorism; weapons of mass destruction
prisoners of war, 86–87

Qaddafi, Muammar, 67
al Qaeda, 77, 78
see also terrorism

Rabin, Yitshak, 51
Rapid Deployment Force, 71
Reagan, Ronald, 59, 60, 61–62, 71
Richman, Sheldon L., 27–28, 52–53
Russia. *See* Soviet Union

Sadat, Anwar, 51, 58–59
see also Egypt
Saikal, Amin, 89
Saudi Arabia
history of American in-

volvement in, 17–18
PLO and, 56
repressive policies of, 56
terrorism in, 77
Twin Pillars foreign policy and, 54–56
U.S. troop deployment to, 13
weapons supplied to by U.S., 56
Schiff, Ze-ev, 61
September 11, 2001, 78–79, 81
Sharon, Ariel, 59–60, 88
Shiism, 64
see also fundamentalist Islamic movement; Islam; Islamic revolution
Shlaim, Avi, 38, 60, 64
Simon, Steven, 86
Sinai Peninsula, 46, 47, 51
Six-Day War, 45–48
Smith, B.J., 22
Somalia, 78
Soviet Union
Afghanistan and, 70
aid to Arab states and, 50
anti-Americanism and, 51, 54
Egypt and, 35–36, 45
Iran and, 30–31
Pan-Arabism and, 43–44
PLO and, 60
policies of, 18–19, 52
Syria and, 41–42
Sowayan, Saad A., 77
Stalin, Joseph, 19
Stern gang, 24
Suez Canal, 16, 17, 51, 52
Suez crisis, 35–40
Suez-Sinai War, 35–40
Syria, 15–16, 41–42, 51, 60, 77
see also Golan Heights

Taliban, 72, 78, 82
Tanzania, 78
Taraki, Noor Mohammad, 70
terrorism
history of, 13
Iran and, 64–68
Iraq and, 84, 86
Lebanon and, 77
Libya and, 67
PLO and, 50–51
Syria and, 77
U.S. policies and, 87–90
war on terror and, 80, 81–82
Thornburg, Max, 18
Transjordan. *See* Jordan
Tripartite Agreement, 38–39
Truman, Harry S., 11, 19, 27
Truman Doctrine, 19, 21, 22
Turkey, 19, 21, 22, 42
Twin Pillars policy, 54–56

Union of Soviet Socialist Republics (USSR). *See* Soviet Union
United Arab Emirates, 54
United Arab Republic, 42, 44
United Nations (UN), 19, 26–27, 46, 52, 69, 73–75
resolutions, 26–27, 46, 48, 52
Special Commissions, 25–26, 75
U.S. policy
arming of Iraq against Iran, 68–70
Israel and, 52, 54
Israel-Palestine mediator role in, 87–88

PICTURE CREDITS

ABOUT THE AUTHOR

Debra A. Miller is a writer and lawyer with an interest in current events and history. She began her law career in Washington, D.C., where she worked on legislative, policy, and legal matters in government, public interest, and private law firm positions. She now lives with her husband in Encinitas, California. She has written and edited numerous publications for legal publishers, as well as books and anthologies on historical and political topics.